Happy

birthday

holidays

new house

countdown

Love

Leslie &

Aundrea

The Miele Cook Book

PRODUCED IN ASSOCIATION WITH
THE GOOD HOUSEKEEPING INSTITUTE

THE MIELE COMPANY LIMITED

Miele would like to acknowledge the help of the
following people during the production of this book.

Editor: Margaret Coombes, assisted by Favell Bevan, GHI
Recipe research and testing: Margaret Alden, Alyson Jones; Home Economists
Copy editor: Barbara Croxford
Photography: Anthony Blake, Good Housekeeping
Melvin Grey – Dinner Party section
John Moffat
Art director: Dan McDonough
Design and typography: Ted Skilbeck, Equinox NRS
Typeset by: House of Naylor
Reproduction by: CRC Limited, London
Printed by: N&W Litho, Truro, Cornwall
Bound by: Robert Hartnoll Limited, Bodmin, Cornwall

Special thanks to:
The Home Economics team at Miele Abingdon
The students and staff of the Home Economics Department Sheffield City
Polytechnic, for initial testing and useful comments on the pilot for this edition

The Miele Cook Book was produced by John Haycock Associates Limited

Copies of this book are available from Miele Company, for £9.95
or the equivalent local currency

British Library
The Miele Cook Book
1. Cookery
I. Good Housekeeping Institute
641.5   TX717

ISBN 0 9509960 0 9

Miele Double oven H809B2.
A selection of Miele hobs, deep fat fryer,
grill and extractors.

CONTENTS

FOREWORD

By Rudolf Miele

The pleasure of cooking is yours. You can delight your family with tempting dishes and your guests, too, will appreciate your culinary arts. To prepare meals with loving care, an imaginative and accomplished cook deserves not only excellent ingredients, but also appliances of superb technical quality.

It has always been our aim to offer the cook versatile, high-performance appliances to ensure that cooking and baking are a pleasure. Our engineers are constantly exploring the latest technological developments in order to produce an advanced oven which is a joy to use. The finest materials are selected in manufacture, to ensure that your cooker or oven gives you long years of enjoyment and satisfaction.

We hope the great variety of recipes in our new cook book will offer you the opportunity of using your cooker to its full potential and of producing mouth-watering meals.

INTRODUCTION

By Good Housekeeping Institute

We at Good Housekeeping are often asked to test this piece of kitchen equipment or that bit of gadgetry. We usually take a look. And so when Miele approached us to co-operate in producing this book, we first took two ovens and a hob into one of our test kitchens so that we could test all the recipes fully, in normal working conditions, to make sure that you would get perfect results every time.

Over the months we grew fond of them, not only for their utter reliability, superb performance, but also for their flexibility, design and craftsmanship. But perhaps even more, we enjoyed the challenge of devising the sort of recipes and dishes that a Miele owner would want to cook.

We hope you will enjoy the recipes we have selected and tested for you. Once you have tried them out, and started to explore the limitless potential of your Miele oven or hob, we hope you will go on to adapt and create your own recipes and dishes.

Miele's Home Economics team have been delighted to have the co-operation of the Good Housekeeping Institute in the compilation of the recipes in this book. In this section, we have tried to answer the questions most frequently put to us about Miele ovens and hobs, and we hope that you will benefit from these tips and hints on how to get the best out of your new appliance.

THE MIELE WAY

When you buy any new cooker, oven or hob, you naturally need to spend some time getting to know it, not only through the instruction book, but also by practical experience. Each one has its own 'personality,' and although the temperatures and settings we give with each recipe in this book have been tested on Miele equipment in Good Housekeeping's test kitchens, and are as accurate as possible, only you will know the individual character of your oven, and only you can make the fine adjustments that may be needed to achieve absolute perfection every time.

Miele ovens provide many different cooking systems to give you perfect results everytime. You can use conventional cooking mode, fan system or automatic roast – and of course you can grill. Some models incorporate an intensive bake setting, excellent for quiches and there is a rôtisserie.

You can easily set your Miele oven to operate automatically, a real boon if you want to eat as soon as you get home. And with the automatic roasting feature on the fan oven, you can cook roasts to perfection every time, whether you're there or not, as this feature seals the joint at a high temperature, and then reverts to a lower temperature automatically.

THE GRILL

Always pre-heat the grill with the oven door closed for about five minutes before starting to cook. The door is kept closed during grilling to save energy.

Most grilling is done at temperatures between 230°C and 275°C. You should use the lower shelves for slower grilling when cooking thicker foods to allow the heat to penetrate more slowly and thus more evenly. When you want to baste food during grilling, do it in the grill pan, and for ease of cleaning, line the pan with kitchen foil.

Fatty foods grill best on the rack over the grill pan. Place the anti-splash tray under the rack to prevent spitting if the temperature is high or the food is close to the grill elements.

You can also use the grill for browning the surface of food that has been cooked in a casserole, for instance cheese-topped pasta dishes or crème brûlée, which need flash-browning. Miele's adjustable shelf depth is especially valuable here: it allows you to position large and deep dishes at the correct distance from the grill elements.

Cooked foods can be kept warm prior to serving at the bottom of the oven whilst you are using the grill.

KEEPING YOUR OVEN CLEAN

To ensure that your Miele oven remains in pristine condition it is important that it is cleaned regularly and correctly.

First of all, it is important to understand which parts of the oven interior will stay clean with just a little help from you, and which areas need to be manually cleaned. Miele ovens are lined with a special catalytic coating on the sides, rear and roof of the oven. The oven floor is of ordinary enamel and the door is composed of glass with an enamelled surround. The shelf supports are made of chrome and are removeable.

Firstly remove the oven trays. Remove the shelf supports at the side of the oven by unscrewing the knurled nuts. These components may be washed by hand using a non-abrasive cleaner or in a dishwasher.

It is now important to clean the parts of the oven interior that are not removeable; i.e. the oven floor and the door. The floor is cleaned using a damp cloth and non-abrasive cleaner. If cleaning is particularly difficult a proprietary oven cleaner may be used. However, the oven cleaner MUST NOT come into contact with any other part of the oven except the floor.

The oven door may be removed (see instruction book). This should be cleaned using a damp cloth and non-abrasive cleaner. Polish with a dry cloth afterwards. NEVER use a wet cloth.

The specially coated catalytic oven liners can only function at a temperature above 200°C. With the oven empty, select a temperature of 240°C and the selector switch at 'Intensive Bake' (if available) or the fan setting. Leave the oven at this setting for at least one hour. If the oven is very heavily soiled it may require a couple of hours. When the recommended time has elapsed, turn the oven switches to 'off.' Leave the oven to cool and then inspect. If the oven is clean, replace the shelf supports and oven trays. If you find a few spots remaining then a little extra cleaning may help. This is done as follows. This process may only be conducted on a COLD oven interior.

In a small bowl add a little mild detergent to some warm water. Using a pot brush, apply the solution to the 'spots' on the oven walls, gently scrubbing. You won't have to spend longer than 5 to 10 minutes doing this. Now put the oven onto clean, as before.

A cleaned oven always looks good, and it is always worth the effort since a clean oven reduces the chances of stale cooking smells from baking and roasting residue.

The outside of the oven must NEVER be cleaned with anything abrasive. Just water and a mild detergent. Polish with a soft cloth and a proprietary polish if desired.

TO KNOW YOUR OVEN

THE OVEN

Always use the handle supplied for lifting the trays and shelves safely from the oven. If you use oven gloves, the type that fit separately on each hand are better than a double mitt, because of the width of the trays and shelves.

When buying new dishes and casseroles for the oven, make use of this extra shelf width. Sometimes a wider, shallower dish is more convenient than a narrow deep one that takes the space of two shelves. However, two smaller containers to fit side-by-side on the shelf can be very practical when cooking a complete meal.

You will find a slightly deeper enamel pan with your oven, which may be used as a roasting pan. You can either roast directly on this, or on the wire rack placed in the pan. You should use the anti-splash tray if roasting at high temperatures.

Cake tins, bread tins and baking sheets should be stood directly on the wire racks in the oven to allow even heat penetration.

As a general rule, you should pre-heat when using the conventional oven or cooking method, however in a few instances in this book this is not necessary, as we have indicated in the instructions at the end of the recipes.

Conversion Chart								
Gas	°F	°C	Gas	°F	°C	Gas	°F	°C
	150	70	1	275	140	6	400	200
	175	80	2	300	150	7	425	220
	210	100	3	325	160	8	450	230
¼	225	110	4	350	180	9	475	240
½	250	120	5	375	190		500	260

If some of your favourite recipes are in old cookery books, use this chart to find the approximate temperature.

FAN OVEN

The fan oven cooks at about 20°C lower than the conventional oven. As a general rule, the higher the temperature required, the greater the difference becomes. The overall cooking time can however sometimes be shortened if the fan oven is pre-heated.

You will find your Miele fan oven ideal for batch baking, and we have included a special section in this book to help you get the most out of your oven. When batch baking and using three trays, you may find that it is necessary to change the positions of the trays to ensure very even browning, or sometimes you may have to leave one tray in the oven a little longer. This usually applies to whole trays of small cakes, biscuits or scones.

As a general rule, you should position trays as follows for baking: 1 tray – 1st runner from bottom; 2 trays –

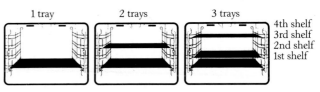

1st and 3rd runners from bottom; 3 trays – 1st, 2nd and 4th runners from bottom.

Scones, vol-au-vent cases and biscuits should be baked directly on the enamel trays supplied, and you can stand bread or cake tins, or casseroles on these trays.

Most dishes cook just as well from a cold start when using the fan oven. When pre-heating is recommended, it is either because foods such as puff pastry and yeast mixtures need instant heat to make them rise quickly, or when the total cooking time is rather short. Again, this has been incorporated in the instructions at the end of each recipe. If however you do not pre-heat, the cooking timed should be extended a little.

When you have a full oven, you should slightly extend the cooking time. However when you are simply baking two cakes at the same time on one shelf, or one above the other, the increase in baking time is minimal.

When roasting in the fan oven, it is important to use the roasting filter, as fat from the roast could be taken into the circulating air in the oven. Remember to remove and wash the filter after use. Do not leave it in place permanently as it will extend baking times by 10-15 minutes. To eliminate fat splashes, you can use a covered roasting dish which will produce very good tender roasts.

Conversion Chart: Conventional Oven/Fan Oven					
Temperature comparisons in °C					
Conventional Oven	Fan Oven	Conventional Oven	Fan Oven	Conventional Oven	Fan Oven
50	50	125	100	200	180
75	70	150	130	225	200
100	90	175	160	250	225

There are occasions when, in the search for perfection to achieve particular results, you may need to use different techniques or methods. A number of the recipes in this book incorporate such changes, and you can use them as a guide for further adaptation of your own favourite recipes. We at Miele will be delighted to help you, so please write to us at: Miele Company Limited, Fairacres, Marcham Road, Abingdon, Oxon OX14 1TW or telephone the Home Economics Department on Abingdon (0235) 554455.

NB In this book, both metric and imperial measures are given. Please use either all metric or all imperial measurements, do not mix them up, as they are not exact equivalents or conversions.

Starters

STARTERS

SPINACH AND CHEESE CREPES

Serves 4

Crêpe batter

125g (4oz) plain flour
1.25ml (¼ level tsp) salt
one egg, beaten
300ml (½ pint) milk
15ml (1 tbsp) vegetable oil
oil or lard, to fry

Filling

125g (4oz) cooked spinach, chopped
225g (8oz) cottage cheese, sieved
25g (1oz) grated Parmesan cheese
5-10ml (1-2 tsp) Worcestershire sauce
salt and pepper
30ml (2 level tbsp) fresh breadcrumbs
25g (1oz) butter, melted

For the batter, sift flour and salt into a bowl. Add the egg and a little of the milk, gradually beat the flour into the liquid, adding the remainder of the milk to make a smooth batter. Stir in the oil. Use the batter to make 8 small crêpes and cook in the oil or melted lard. Stack the crêpes on a plate until all are ready. For the filling, mix together the spinach, cottage cheese, 15g (½oz) of the Parmesan, the Worcestershire sauce and seasoning. Put the filling on to each crêpe. Fold the sides over the filling, then roll up and arrange seamside down in a buttered au gratin dish. Scatter the breadcrumbs and remaining Parmesan over the crêpes and pour the melted butter over evenly. Bake in the oven for about 15 minutes, until the surface is browned and crisp.

Oven	Conventional	Fan
Temperature	200°C	180°C
Preheating	Recommended	Recommended
Shelf position	3rd	1st
Time	15-20 minutes	10-15 minutes

SALMON PATE

Serves 6

25g (1oz) butter
25g (1oz) plain flour
200ml (7½ floz) milk
good pinch of powdered bay leaf
salt and pepper
125g (4oz) fresh haddock, skinned and boned
225g (8oz) fresh salmon, skinned and boned
finely grated rind and juice of 1 small lemon
7.5ml (½ tbsp) chopped fresh parsley
one egg, beaten
25g (1oz) butter, melted
thin cucumber slices, to garnish

Butter six individual soufflé dishes. Melt the butter in a saucepan, stir in the flour and cook gently without browning for 1-2 minutes. Remove the pan from the heat and gradually stir in the milk. Bring to the boil, stirring, and cook for 2-3 minutes until thickened. Add the bay and seasoning to taste. Process or mince the haddock and salmon very finely – this is important for a smooth pâté. Mix the fish, lemon rind and juice, parsley and egg thoroughly into the sauce. Divide the mixture between the soufflé dishes and drizzle the melted butter over each one. Put the dishes into a roasting tin (bain marie) and pour in sufficient hot water to come halfway up sides of the dishes. Bake in the oven for about 25 minutes, until the pâté is just firm to the touch. Remove from the tin, leave to cool. Cover and chill in the refrigerator. Garnish with thin cucumber slices and serve with melba toast.

Oven	Conventional	Fan
Temperature	170°C	150°C
Preheating	Recommended	Not necessary
Shelf position	1st	1st
Time	25-30 minutes	20-25 minutes

CHICKEN LIVER PATE WITH GREEN PEPPERCORNS

Serves 8

125g (4oz) butter
125g (4oz) onion, roughly chopped
450g (1lb) chicken livers
1 garlic clove, skinned and crushed
2.5ml (½ level tsp) dried marjoram
freshly ground pepper
7.5ml (1½ level tsp) salt
5ml (1 tsp) lemon juice
15ml (1 tbsp) sherry
45-60ml (3-4 tbsp) single cream
10ml (2 level tsp) chopped green peppercorns

Prepare a day ahead. Melt 50g (2oz) of the butter in a frying pan and fry the onion without colouring until softened. Add the livers, garlic, marjoram, pepper, salt, lemon juice and sherry. Cook over a gentle heat for about 10 minutes, until the livers firm and change colour. Put into blender with the cream and purée until smooth, or push through a metal sieve. Stir in the peppercorns. Adjust the seasoning, turn into a serving dish. The mixture should come to just below the rim. Refrigerate until firm, at least 2 hours. Melt the remaining butter, skim and spoon over the pâté. Refrigerate to set. Leave at room temperature for 30 minutes before serving. Serve with melba or fresh toast.

PASTA VERDI WITH WALNUT SAUCE

Serves 4

175g (6oz) tagliatelle or spaghetti verdi
salt and pepper
150ml (¼ pint) single cream
75g (3oz) walnuts, chopped
one large garlic clove, skinned and crushed
5ml (1 tsp) lemon juice

Cook the tagliatelle or spaghetti in a saucepan of boiling salted water for about 10 minutes until just tender. Drain and keep warm.

Put the cream into a pan and heat gently. Add the walnuts, garlic, lemon juice and seasoning, stir well and heat through. Serve the pasta on warmed individual dishes and spoon the sauce over.

BAKED EGGS

Serves 8

25g (1oz) butter
8 eggs
salt and pepper
120ml (4floz) double or single cream
chopped fresh parsley, to garnish

Butter 8 small cocotte dishes, stand them in a roasting tin. Heat in the oven for 3 minutes. Break an egg into each cocotte, sprinkle with salt and pepper and spoon cream over each one. Pour sufficient hot water into the tin to come halfway up sides of the cocottes. Bake in the oven for about 12 minutes, until the eggs are just set. Sprinkle with chopped parsley and serve immediately with fingers of toast.

Oven	Conventional	Fan
Temperature	170°C	150°C
Preheating	Recommended	Recommended
Shelf position	4th	4th
Time	12-15 minutes	9-12 minutes

Right: Pasta Verdi with Walnut Sauce

BAKED STUFFED AVOCADOS

Serves 4

2 avocados
2 spring onions, trimmed
one 198g (7oz) can sweetcorn kernels with peppers, drained
60ml (4 tbsp) single cream
5-10ml (1-2 tsp) lemon juice
few drops of Tabasco sauce
pinch of chilli powder
salt and pepper
chopped fresh parsley, to garnish

Cut the avocados in half, twist to separate the halves and remove stones. Scoop out the flesh, keeping the skins intact. Process or finely chop the spring onions, add the avocado flesh and process or mash smooth. Mix in the sweetcorn with peppers and the cream. Add the lemon juice, Tabasco, chilli powder and seasoning to taste. Fill the avocado shells with the mixture, arrange in an ovenproof dish and bake in the oven for about 15 minutes until heated through. Sprinkle chopped parsley over and serve hot with melba toast.

Oven	Conventional	Fan
Temperature	190°C	170°C
Preheating	Recommended	Recommended
Shelf position	1st	1st
Time	20-25 minutes	15 minutes

DEEP FRIED MUSHROOMS WITH TANGY SAUCE

Serves 6

225g (8oz) cup mushrooms, wiped
Batter
50g (2oz) plain flour
1.25ml (¼ level tsp) salt
75ml (2½floz) warm water
one egg white
oil for deep frying
Sauce
one small onion, finely chopped
one garlic clove, skinned and crushed
15ml (1 tbsp) vegetable oil
5ml (1 level tsp) soft brown sugar
15ml (1 tbsp) Worcestershire sauce
one 225g (8oz) can tomatoes
5ml (1 level tsp) tomato purée
1.25ml (¼ level tsp) dried basil
salt and pepper

Remove the mushroom stalks. For the batter, sift the flour and salt into a bowl. Beat in the warm water. Whisk the egg white until softly stiff and fold into the flour mixture. Heat the oil to 180°C or when a small cube of bread browns in about half a minute. Spear each mushroom on a skewer, dip into the batter to coat evenly then push off the skewer into the heated oil a few at a time. Fry for 2-3 minutes until golden. Drain on absorbent kitchen paper. Meanwhile for the sauce, heat the oil in a pan and cook the onion and garlic until softened but not brown. Mix in the sugar, sauce, tomatoes, purée, basil and seasoning. Bring to the boil and cook for about 5 minutes until thick and no liquid remains. Serve the mushrooms immediately with the sauce.

STARTERS

AUBERGINES A LA GRECQUE

Serves 4

one large aubergine, about 350g (12oz)
45ml (3 tbsp) vegetable oil
15ml (1 tbsp) olive oil
150ml (¼ pint) dry white wine
150ml (¼ pint) water
30ml (2 tbsp) lemon juice
one garlic clove, skinned and crushed
one small bay leaf
parsley sprig
salt and pepper
chopped fresh parsley, to garnish

Halve the aubergine and cut in slices. Degorge the aubergine slices by sprinkling with salt and leaving for 1 hour to extract the juices. Rinse well in cold water and pat dry with absorbent kitchen paper. Put the oils, wine, water, lemon juice, garlic, bay leaf, parsley sprig and seasoning into a pan. Bring to the boil, then stir in the aubergine slices. Cover and cook for about 10 minutes, until the aubergine is just tender. Turn into a dish to cool and remove the bay leaf and parsley sprig. Serve the aubergine slices with the juices, sprinkle with chopped parsley and accompany with brown bread.

PRAWNS IN ASPIC

Serves 6

one 28g (1oz) packet aspic powder
30ml (2 tbsp) medium dry sherry
15ml (1 tbsp) lemon juice
salt and pepper
one 225g (8oz) packet prawns, thawed
one egg, hard-boiled, sliced

Dissolve the aspic powder in 45ml (3 tbsp) less water than packet instructions recommend, using a pan on low hob heat. Cool. Stir the sherry and lemon juice into the liquid aspic and season to taste. Pick over the prawns and pat dry with absorbent kitchen paper. Divide the prawns between six 150ml (¼ pint) individual soufflé dishes and spoon over three-quarters of the liquid aspic jelly. Refrigerate to set. Garnish the prawn jellies with slices of hard-boiled egg and spoon over the remaining liquid aspic. Refrigerate again to set. Leave the dishes at room temperature for about 20 minutes before serving. Serve with wafer thin slices of brown bread and butter. Note: Canned consommé can be used as an alternative to the aspic. Test the set after chilling – it should just hold its shape. If not firm enough, add 5ml (1 level tsp) gelatine dissolved in 15ml (1 tbsp) water.

Celery and Cheese Soup

CELERY AND CHEESE SOUP

Serves 6

40g (1½oz) butter or margarine
175g (6oz) celery, washed, trimmed and finely chopped
45ml (3 level tbsp) plain flour
300ml (½ pint) milk
600ml (1 pint) light stock
50g (2oz) grated mature Cheddar cheese
50g (2oz) grated Stilton cheese
salt and pepper

Melt the butter in a saucepan and gently fry the celery for 5 minutes without colouring. Stir in the flour and cook for 2 minutes. Stir in the milk and stock and bring to the boil. Cover and simmer for 15 minutes or until the celery is tender, stirring several times. Gradually add the cheeses and stir until melted. Add seasoning to taste and reheat gently. Serve with toast.

FRESH TOMATO SOUP

Serves 6

50g (2oz) butter or margarine
175g (6oz) onion, finely sliced
900g (2lb) tomatoes
45ml (3 level tbsp) plain flour
900ml (1½ pints) chicken stock
30ml (2 level tbsp) tomato purée
2.5ml (½ level tsp) dried basil or 5ml (1 level tsp) chopped fresh basil
salt and pepper
150ml (¼ pint) single cream

Melt the butter in a medium saucepan and gently fry the onion until golden brown. Meanwhile wipe and halve tomatoes, scoop out the seeds into a sieve placed over the bowl. Press the seeds to remove all the tomato pulp and juice; discard the seeds, reserve the juice. Remove the pan from the heat, stir in the flour, stock, tomato purée, herbs and seasoning, mixing well. Bring to the boil, stirring all the time. Add the tomatoes with reserved juice, cover the pan and simmer gently for about 30 minutes. Cool slightly. Purée the tomato mixture a little at a time in a blender. Strain through a nylon sieve into a clean pan and reheat. Adjust the seasoning and ladle the soup into individual soup cups. Swirl a little cream through each bowl just before serving.

PUREE OF PARSNIP SOUP

Serves 6

40g (1½oz) butter or margarine
125g (4oz) onion, sliced
700g (1½lb) parsnips, peeled and finely diced
5ml (1 level tsp) curry powder
2.5ml (½ level tsp) ground cumin
1.4 litres (2½ pints) light stock
salt and pepper

Melt the butter in a large saucepan and fry the onion and parsnips for about 3 minutes. Stir in the curry powder and cumin and fry for a further 2 minutes. Add the stock, bring to the boil, reduce the heat, cover and simmer for about 45 minutes, until the vegetables are tender. Cool slightly, then use a slotted draining spoon to transfer the vegetables to a blender. Add a little stock and purée until smooth. Return to the pan. Adjust the seasoning and reheat to serving temperature.

Top: Buttered Asparagus Bottom: Moules Marinières

STARTERS

BUTTERED ASPARAGUS

Serves 6

about 36 asparagus stalks
salt
125g (4oz) butter, melted

Rinse the asparagus carefully to remove any dirt. Scrape the stalks with a potato peeler or knife to remove any scale-like pieces. Cut off the woody ends and make the stalks roughly the same length. Tie into neat bundles of six or eight stalks. Pour enough water into a large deep saucepan to three-quarters cover the stalks. Add 5ml (1 level tsp) salt and bring to the boil. Wedge the asparagus bundles upright in the pan and cover the tips with foil. Simmer gently for about 10 minutes, until the asparagus is just tender. The stalks will be poached and the delicate tips gently steamed; the point of a knife should slip easily into the bottom part of the stalk. Lift the bundles carefully out of the water, drain and place on a serving plate; remove the string. Cover with buttered greaseproof and foil and keep warm in a slow oven. Serve the asparagus with the melted butter.

Note: An unusual alternative to asparagus is seakale. It can be cooked in the same way and has a good, nutty taste.

BROAD BEANS AND HAM MAYONNAISE

Serves 4

450g (1lb) fresh broad beans, shelled, or one 227g (8oz) packet frozen, thawed
salt and pepper
15ml (1 tbsp) vegetable oil
7.5ml (½ tbsp) vinegar
1.25ml (¼ level tsp) dried thyme
45ml (3 level tbsp) mayonnaise
25ml (1½ tbsp) single cream
2-3 spring onions, trimmed and finely chopped
50g (2oz) ham, cut in matchsticks
crisp lettuce leaves, to serve

Cook the beans in a saucepan of boiling salted water for 4-5 minutes or until just tender. Drain. Immediately whisk together the oil, vinegar, thyme and seasoning. Stir in the hot beans. Allow to cool. Stir the mayonnaise, cream, spring onions and ham into the beans. Arrange lettuce leaves on small serving plates, pile the bean mixture on to them.

MOULES MARINIERES

Serves 4

4 dozen mussels, about 3.4 litres (6 pints)
butter
4 shallots or 1 medium onion, finely chopped
½ bottle dry white wine
chopped fresh parsley
2 thyme sprigs, if available, or a light sprinkling of dried thyme
one bay leaf
freshly ground pepper
10ml (2 level tsp) plain flour

Put the mussels in a large bowl and, under running cold water, scrape off the mud, barnacles, seaweed and 'beards' with a small sharp knife. Discard any that are open or even just loose (unless a tap on the shell makes them close), or any that are cracked. Rinse again until there is no trace of sand in the bowl. Melt a large knob of butter in a saucepan and fry the shallots until soft but not coloured. Add the wine, a small handful of chopped parsley, the thyme, bay leaf and several turns of pepper from the mill. Cover and simmer for 10 minutes. Add the drained mussels, a handful at a time. Cover and 'steam', for about 5 minutes, shaking often, until the shells open. Holding the mussels over the pan to catch the juices, remove the top shells, and place mussels in warmed wide soup plates. Keep warm. Strain the liquor and boil fast to reduce by half. Thicken it a little by whisking in a small knob of soft butter creamed with the flour.

Pâtés & Terrines

PATE DE CAMPAGNE WITH BLACK OLIVES

Serves 8 as a main dish

450g (1lb) belly pork, rinded and boned
275g (10oz) pie veal, trimmed
175g (6oz) lamb's liver
175g (6oz) onion, quartered
one garlic clove, skinned and crushed
salt and pepper
5ml (1 level tsp) dried sage
30ml (2 tbsp) vegetable oil
15ml (1 tbsp) lemon juice
75g (3oz) black olives, stoned and roughly chopped
30ml (2 tbsp) brandy
275g (10oz) streaky bacon rashers, rinded and halved

Process or finely mince the pork, veal, liver and onion. Mix with the garlic, salt and pepper, sage, oil, lemon juice, olives and brandy. Arrange the bacon rashers overlapping across the base of the terrine. Spread a layer of the minced mixture over them. Continue filling with two more layers each of bacon and meat mixture finishing with bacon. Press buttered foil on top to overlap the sides of the terrine. Cover with the lid. Put terrine into the baking tin and pour in sufficient hot water to come a third of the way up sides of the terrine. Bake in the oven for about 1¾ hours. When cooked, remove from the bain marie. Pour off the juices and, when cold, scrape away any fat. Heat the juices and spoon over the terrine. Replace the foil, lay a piece of cardboard cut to fit the top on the terrine. Place weights on top. Chill in the refrigerator. Leave at room temperature for 30 minutes before serving. Accompany the thickly cut terrine with bread, toast and salad.

Oven	Conventional	Fan
Temperature	170°C	150°C
Preheating	Not necessary	Not necessary
Shelf position	1st	1st
Time	2 hours	1¾ hours

DUCK AND ORANGE TERRINE

Serves 6 as main meal

1.8kg (4lb) oven-ready duckling
350g (12oz) belly of pork, skin removed
125g (4oz) lamb's liver
125g (4oz) onion
2 oranges
one garlic clove, skinned and crushed
5ml (1 level tsp) salt
freshly ground pepper
2.5ml (½ level tsp) ground mace
15ml (1 level tbsp) chopped fresh parsley
30ml (2 tbsp) sherry
300ml (½ pint) liquid aspic jelly
celery leaves, to garnish

Prepare two days ahead. Discard the skin and fat layer from the duckling. Cut away the breast portion. Remove the rest of the flesh, about 350g (12oz). Finely mince the duckling flesh, except the breast, with the pork, liver and onion. Grate in the rind of one orange. Segment the flesh of this orange, free of membrane, over a bowl to collect any juice. Cut the segments into small pieces. Combine the meats, except the breast meat, orange juice, orange pieces, garlic, seasoning, mace, parsley and sherry. Press half mixture into a 1.1 litre (2 pint) terrine. Lay the breast portions on top and spread the remaining mixture over. Cover with foil and the lid. Place the dish in a roasting tin (bain marie) and pour in sufficient hot water to come halfway up the sides of the terrine. Bake in the oven for about 2¾ hours, until the meat is tender and shrinking from the sides of the tin. Weight down and refrigerate until cold. Scrape off any solidified fat and drain away juices. Garnish with the remaining orange, sliced, and celery leaves. Spoon over the aspic when nearly set. Chill in the refrigerator. Leave at room temperature for 30 minutes before serving.

Oven	Conventional	Fan
Temperature	170°C	150°C
Preheating	Not necessary	Not necessary
Shelf position	1st	1st
Time	3 hours	2¾ hours

PATES AND TERRINES

POTTED CHICKEN WITH TARRAGON

Serves 4-6 as a main dish

1.4kg (3lb) oven-ready chicken
45ml (3 tbsp) dry sherry
300ml (½ pint) stock
15ml (1 level tbsp) chopped fresh tarragon or 5ml (1 level tsp) dried
50g (2oz) butter
one onion, chopped
one carrot, peeled and chopped
salt and pepper
5-10ml (1-2 tsp) lemon juice
fresh tarragon leaves, to garnish

The day before, place the prepared chicken in a flameproof casserole with the sherry, stock, tarragon, butter, onion, carrot and seasoning. Cover tightly and cook in the oven for about 1¼ hours, until the chicken is tender. Lift the chicken out of the casserole, cut off all the flesh, reserving the skin and bones. Coarsely mince the chicken meat. Return the skin and broken-up bones to the casserole. Boil the contents rapidly until the liquid has reduced to 225ml (8fl oz). Strain, reserving the juices. Mix the minced chicken, lemon juice and reserved juices together and adjust the seasoning. Pack into small dishes, cover and chill well. Leave at a cool room temperature for 30 minutes before serving. Garnish with fresh tarragon leaves.

Oven	Conventional	Fan
Temperature	180°C	160°C
Preheating	Not necessary	Not necessary
Shelf position	1st	1st
Time	1½ hours	1¼ hours

COARSE GARLIC PATE

Serves 8-10 as a main dish

450g (1lb) ox liver
60ml (4 tbsp) milk
450g (1lb) belly pork
225g (8oz) pork fat
225g (8oz) stewing steak
125g (4oz) onion
125g (4oz) mushrooms, wiped
4 garlic cloves
45ml (3 tbsp) red wine
1.25ml (¼ level tsp) ground nutmeg
7.5ml (1½ level tsp) salt
milled pepper
225g (8oz) lean bacon rashers, rinded

Make pâté two days before needed. Soak the liver in the milk for about 1 hour, drain. Mince the liver, pork, pork fat, steak and onion. Roughly chop the mushrooms and stir into the minced mixture. Crush the garlic and add to the pâté ingredients along with the wine, nutmeg and seasonings. Use a 1.4 litre (2½ pint) oval pie dish. Arrange bacon rashers across the base and up sides of the terrine. Pack mixture tightly into the dish. Cover with foil and put the pie dish into a roasting tin half filled with boiling water (bain marie) and cook in the oven until the meat is tender and shrinking from the sides of the dish. When cooked, take dish out of the tin and put weights on to the pâté. Refrigerate until required. Turn out and let pâté come to for 30 minutes at room temperature before serving.

Oven	Conventional	Fan
Temperature	170°C	150°C
Preheating	Not necessary	Not necessary
Shelf position	1st	1st
Time	2 hours	1¾ hours

Right: Coarse Garlic Pâté

PATES AND TERRINES

POTTED RABBIT

Serves 8 as a main dish

900g (2lb) rabbit pieces or
350g (12oz) boneless rabbit meat
450g (1lb) belly pork, boned and skinned
225g (8oz) streaky bacon, rinded
grated rind of half a lemon
30ml (2 tbsp) lemon juice
60ml (4 tbsp) brandy
5ml (1 level tsp) salt
freshly ground pepper
5ml (1 level tsp) crushed juniper berries
2 eggs
150ml (¼ pint) single cream
parsley

Two days ahead, if necessary, bone the rabbit to give 350g (12oz) meat. Cut half of the rabbit meat into very small pieces. Coarsely mince the remainder. Finely mince the belly pork and bacon together. Combine all the meats with the lemon rind, lemon juice, brandy, salt and pepper. Tie the juniper berries in muslin and push into the meat. Cover and leave in the refrigerator overnight. Remove the muslin bag. Beat the eggs and cream into the meats until thoroughly mixed. Pack into 8 large ramekin dishes and cover with foil. Place in a roasting tin (bain marie) and pour in sufficient hot water to come halfway up the sides of the dishes. Bake in the oven for about 1¾ hours, until the meat is tender and shrinking from the sides of the dishes. Weight down and leave overnight in the refrigerator. Leave at room temperature for 30 minutes before serving. Garnish with parsley.

Oven	Conventional	Fan
Temperature	150°C	130°C
Preheating	Not necessary	Not necessary
Shelf position	1st	1st
Time	2 hours	1¾ hours

VEAL, WINE AND APRICOT PATE

Serves 6 as a main dish

700g (1½lb) pie veal, trimmed
25g (1oz) dried apricots
100ml (4floz) dry white wine
225g (8oz) pork fat
half a small bunch of watercress, washed and trimmed
2 garlic cloves, skinned and crushed
2 eggs
50g (2oz) fresh white breadcrumbs
2.5ml (½ level tsp) ground allspice
7.5ml (1½ level tsp) salt
freshly ground pepper

Two days ahead, roughly cut up the pie veal and place with apricots in a shallow dish. Pour over the wine. Cover and leave overnight in the refrigerator. Drain, reserving the marinade. Finely mince the veal and apricots with the pork fat. Chop half the watercress, reserve the rest for garnish. In a large mixing bowl, combine all the ingredients, including the marinade. Mix well. Spoon the mixture into a 1.4 litre (2½ pint) loaf tin, press down well. Cover with foil, place in a roasting tin (bain marie) and pour in sufficient hot water to come half way up the sides of the tin. Cook in the oven for about 1½ hours, until the meat is tender and shrinking from the sides of the tin. Remove the pâté from roasting tin, spoon off excess fat. Leave to cool slightly then cover with greaseproof paper and weight down overnight. Turn out, wrap and refrigerate. Leave at room temperature for 30 minutes before serving. Garnish with the remaining watercress sprigs.

Oven	Conventional	Fan
Temperature	170°C	150°C
Preheating	Not necessary	Not necessary
Shelf position	1st	1st
Time	1¾ hours	1½ hours

CHEESE AND NUT ROAST

Serves 4-6

50g (2oz) butter
125g (4oz) onion, chopped
50g (2oz) hazelnuts, finely chopped
50g (2oz) Brazil nuts, finely chopped
125g (4oz) unsalted peanuts, finely chopped
125g (4oz) fresh brown breadcrumbs
2 eggs
175g (6oz) Sage Derby cheese or mild Cheddar cheese with 5ml (1 level tsp) rubbed sage, finely grated
salt and pepper
15ml (1 level tbsp) plain flour
300ml (½ pint) milk

Melt 25g (1oz) of the butter in a saucepan and fry the onion until golden brown. Stir together the nuts, onion, breadcrumbs, eggs, 125g (4oz) of the cheese and sage if required, season to taste. Grease and base line a 900ml (1½ pint) loaf tin. Press the nut mixture evenly into the tin. Bake in the oven for about 35 minutes until golden brown. Leave to cool in the tin for 2-3 minutes before turning out. Meanwhile, melt the remaining butter in a small saucepan, stir in the flour and cook, stirring, for 1 minute. Remove the pan from the heat and gradually stir in the milk. Bring to the boil, stirring, and cook for 1 minute until thickened. Remove from the heat and stir in the remaining grated cheese. Season. Serve hot with the Cheese and Nut Roast.

Oven	Conventional	Fan
Temperature	180°C	160°C
Preheating	Not necessary	Not necessary
Shelf position	1st	1st
Time	45 minutes	35 minutes

HADDOCK PATE EN CROUTE

Serves 6 as a main dish

50g (2oz) butter
350g (12oz) smoked haddock fillet, skinned
30ml (2 tbsp) lemon juice
175g (6oz) cream cheese
2 eggs
freshly ground pepper
shortcrust pastry, made with 175g (6oz) plain flour
2 caps canned pimento, well drained
50g (2oz) capers, chopped
chopped fresh parsley

A day ahead, melt the butter in a frying pan and gently fry the haddock for about 5 minutes, or until beginning to flake, turning once. Place the fish and cooking juices in a bowl. Cool slightly. Flake the fish, discarding the bones and beat in the lemon juice, cheese, one egg and pepper to taste. It is unlikely that salt will be needed. Leave to cool completely. Meanwhile, roll out the pastry thinly and use three-quarters to line a 750ml (1¼ pint) oblong foil dish. Split open the pimento caps and place over the pastry base. Sprinkle the capers on top. Spoon the fish mixture into the pastry case. Scatter over a good layer of parsley and top with the remaining pastry, sealing the edges well. Glaze with remaining beaten egg. Stand the foil dish on a hot baking tray. Bake in the oven for about 30 minutes, until well browned.

Oven	Conventional	Fan
Temperature	200°C	180°C
Preheating	Recommended	Recommended
Shelf position	1st	1st
Time	40 minutes	30 minutes

Top: Mustard Beef Ring & Veal and Ham Raised Pie Bottom: Haddock Pâté en Croûte

MUSTARD BEEF RING

Serves 8

| 350g (12oz) onion |
| 225g (8oz) salami, sliced |
| 700g (1½lb) lean minced beef |
| 175g (6oz) fresh brown breadcrumbs |
| 5ml (1 level tsp) ground nutmeg |
| 20ml (4 level tsp) whole grain mustard |
| 2 eggs, beaten |
| 5ml (1 level tsp) salt |
| freshly ground pepper |
| 30ml (2 tbsp) tomato ketchup mixed with |
| 5ml (1 level tsp) soy sauce, to glaze |

Mince the onion and salami coarsely. Combine with the remaining ingredients except the tomato ketchup and soy sauce, stir well until evenly blended. Press into a greased 1.1 litre (2 pint) ring mould and cover with foil. Place on a baking tray and bake in the oven for about 1 hour until firm and slightly shrunk from the sides of the ring. Turn out of the tin, cool a little and coat evenly with the glaze. Serve hot or cold, with a cucumber and tomato garnish.

Oven	Conventional	Fan
Temperature	180°C	160°C
Preheating	Not necessary	Not necessary
Shelf position	1st	1st
Time	1¼ hours	1 hour

VEAL AND HAM RAISED PIE

Serves 8-10

| 450g (1lb) minced veal |
| 125g (4oz) minced ham |
| 30ml (2 level tbsp) chopped parsley |
| 2.5ml (½ level tsp) ground mace |
| 1.25ml (¼ level tsp) ground bayleaves |
| grated rind of 1 lemon |
| 225g (8oz) onion |
| salt and pepper |
| 125g (4oz) lard |
| 350g (12oz) wholemeal flour |
| one egg yolk |
| 3 hard-boiled eggs |

Lard and base line a 1.4 litre (2½ pint) loaf tin. Combine the first six ingredients, then add the finely chopped onion. 5ml (1 level tsp) salt, and 1.25ml (¼ level tsp) milled pepper. Gently melt the lard in 200ml (7floz) water. Bring to the boil, tip in the flour with 2.5ml (½ level tsp) salt and beat well. Beat in the egg yolk. Cool, covered, until manageable. Pat two-thirds of the pastry into the prepared tin to line it evenly. Press in half the meat mixture, place the shelled eggs down the centre. Fill with the remaining mixture. Cover with the remaining pastry, decorate with trimmings, make 2-3 small holes on top. Bake in the oven for about 1 hour covering towards the end of cooking time if necessary to prevent over-browning. Cool completely. Fill with a little nearly-set aspic jelly if wished. Let set. Turn out of tin for serving. Garnish with radishes.

Oven	Conventional	Fan
Temperature	180°C	160°C
Preheating	Recommended	Not necessary
Shelf position	1st	1st
Time	1¼ hours	1 hour

RILLETTES OF PORK

Serves 8 as a main dish

| 15ml (1 level tbsp) salt |
| 900g (2lb) belly pork, skin and bones removed |
| 450g (1lb) pork fat |
| freshly ground pepper |
| 2 bay leaves |
| bouquet garni |
| 75ml (5 tbsp) water |

Two days ahead, rub the salt all over the belly pork and leave covered in the refrigerator overnight. Cut the belly pork along the grain of the meat into thin strips. Cut these into 4cm (1½ inch) lengths. Roughly cut up the pork fat. Put the belly, fat, plenty of pepper, bay leaves and bouquet garni in a casserole. Add the water. Cover and bake in the oven for about 3¾ hours, until the meat is tender. Stir the meat every hour to prevent it sticking. Strain the meat, chill the reserved juices. Using two forks, shred the belly pork. Discard the remaining pieces of fat. Skim the fat from the chilled meat juices. (The juices can be used to enrich soups and casseroles). Melt this fat and mix with the pork. Spoon into 8 ramekin dishes. Refrigerate to set. Leave at a cool room temperature for about 30 minutes before serving.

Oven	Conventional	Fan
Temperature	150°C	130°C
Preheating	Not necessary	Not necessary
Shelf position	1st	1st
Time	4 hours	3¾ hours

Light Meals

BARBECUE PORK

Serves 4

4 pork chops
2.5ml (½ level tsp) salt
2.5ml (½ level tsp) pepper
2.5ml (½ level tsp) caster sugar
2.5ml (½ level tsp) ground ginger
25g (1oz) butter

Barbecue Sauce

10ml (2 tsp) chilli sauce
15ml (1 tbsp) Worcestershire sauce
10ml (2 level tsp) caster sugar
30ml (2 tbsp) vinegar · 5ml (1 tsp) soy sauce
30ml (2 tbsp) tomato ketchup
2 garlic cloves, skinned and crushed
2 bay leaves

Trim the pork chops carefully. Mix together the salt, pepper, sugar and ginger and rub over the chops. Melt the butter in a flame proof casserole and fry the chops, turning them once to brown on both sides. Meanwhile, mix together thoroughly all the ingredients for the barbecue sauce. When the chops are brown , pour off all the fat from the casserole, pour the sauce over. Cook in the oven for about 20 minutes, turning the chops over once. Arrange them on a warmed serving dish and spoon the sauce over.

Oven	Conventional	Fan
Temperature	190°C	170°C
Preheating	Recommended	Not necessary
Shelf position	3rd	3rd
Time	25-30 minutes	20-25 minutes

SMOKED HADDOCK SCRAMBLE

Serves 2

125g (4oz) smoked haddock fillet
3 eggs
30ml (2 tbsp) milk
salt and pepper
5ml (1 tsp) lemon juice
15ml (1 tbsp) double cream
croûtons of fried bread
15g (½oz) butter or margarine
ground paprika

Coarsely flake the fish discarding the black skin and any bone. In a bowl gently whisk together the eggs, milk, seasoning, lemon juice and cream. Make croûtons

from one large slice of bread per person. Remove crusts and fry in shallow oil until golden on each side. Cut each into 6 squares and keep warm. Melt butter in a saucepan and add the egg mixture with the fish. Cook slowly stirring gently and continuously until the egg mixture becomes very creamy in texture. Adjust seasoning then remove from the heat to prevent overcooking. Line a shallow serving dish with freshly made croûtons. Spoon over haddock scramble and serve at once, sprinkled with paprika.

BRUNCH GRILL

Serves 4

8 chipolata sausages
8 bacon rashers, rinded
4 tomatoes, halved
salt and pepper
a little caster sugar
one small aubergine, sliced
30-45ml (2-3 tbsp) vegetable oil
4 eggs
knob of lard

Additions

sautéed potatoes
fried mushrooms
fried bread or fried rice

Place the wire rack on the grill pan and using the anti-splash tray. Arrange sausages, bacon rashers, tomato halves on the rack. Sprinkle tomatoes with salt, pepper and sugar. Turn aubergine slices in the oil and add to the rack. Grill for 4 minutes. Turn over the sausages, bacon and aubergine slices. Grill for 3 minutes. Serve the bacon, aubergine and tomatoes, grill the sausages for 1 minute more to brown if needed. Melt the lard in a frying pan to cover the base. Break the eggs into the pan, baste with the fat. Fry for 2-3 minutes as required.

Grill	
Temperature	275°C
Preheating	Recommended
Shelf position	3rd or 4th
Time	6-8 minutes

Top: Brunch Grill Bottom: Smoked Haddock Scramble

Savoury Rice

SAVOURY RICE

Serves 4

50g (2oz) margarine
one onion, chopped
125g (4oz) long grain rice
175g (6oz) lean cooked gammon rasher, cubed
175g (6oz) golden fillets (whiting), cooked and flaked
one 425g (15oz) can tomatoes
5ml (1 level tsp) turmeric
226g (8oz) packet frozen sweetcorn, peas and peppers
salt and pepper
chopped parsley to garnish

Melt the margarine in a large frying pan and fry the onion for 5 minutes until softened. Add the rice and fry for 2 minutes. Stir in the gammon, whiting, tomatoes and turmeric and simmer gently for 20 minutes. If necessary add a little water during cooking to keep the mixture moist. Stir in the vegetables and seasoning, bring back to the boil and simmer gently for a further 3-4 minutes. Sprinkle the savoury rice with the freshly chopped parsley just before serving.

GRILLED HADDOCK WITH CUCUMBER SAUCE

Serves 4

½ cucumber, de-seeded and coarsely grated
four 175g (6oz) portions haddock or cod fillet
30ml (2 level tbsp) plain flour
salt and pepper
50g (2oz) butter, melted
Sauce
25g (1oz) butter
20g (¾oz) plain flour
300ml (½ pint) milk
15ml (1 tbsp) chopped fresh parsley
25-30 (1½-2 tbsp) lemon juice

Drain the grated cucumber on absorbent kitchen paper. Coat the cod or haddock portions in the flour, salt and pepper. Turn each one thoroughly in the butter, place on the rack over the grill pan. Grill until the fish is golden brown and flakes easily. For the sauce, melt the butter in a saucepan, stir in the flour and heat gently for 1-2 minutes without colouring. Remove the pan from the heat and gradually stir in the milk. Bring to the boil, stirring, and cook for 1 minute until thickened. Add the drained cucumber, parsley, lemon juice and seasoning to taste. Serve the fish and sauce separately.

Grill	
Temperature	260°C
Preheating	Recommended
Shelf position	3rd
Time	10-12 minutes

CAULIFLOWER WITH GARLIC AND BACON

Serves 3-4

one medium cauliflower
salt and pepper
50g (2oz) butter
30ml (2 tbsp) olive oil
one small onion, finely sliced
one garlic clove, skinned and crushed
8 streaky bacon rashers, chopped
30ml (2 tbsp) fresh breadcrumbs
15ml (1 tbsp) chopped fresh parsley

Divide the cauliflower into walnut-sized florets and place in a saucepan. Just cover with boiling water, add salt, bring to the boil and simmer for 2 minutes. Drain well. Using the same saucepan, heat 25g (1oz) of the butter with the oil and cook the onion and garlic for about 5 minutes to soften. Add the bacon and cook for a further 5 minutes. Add the rest of the butter and, when melted, stir in the breadcrumbs and parsley. Cook for a further 1-2 minutes. Place the drained cauliflower in a gratin dish and spoon the breadcrumb mixture evenly on top. Bake in the oven for about 10 minutes, after about 5 minutes cooking time baste with the buttery juices in the dish. When ready, the cauliflower should be tender but still firm. Before serving, sprinkle with pepper.

Oven	Conventional	Fan
Temperature	190°C	170°C
Preheating	Recommended	Not necessary
Shelf position	3rd	3rd
Time	10-15 minutes	10-15 minutes

COD WITH CORIANDER IN CREAM
Serves 4

550g (1¼lb) thick cut cod fillet, skinned
30ml (2 level tbsp) plain flour
10ml (2 level tsp) ground coriander
salt and pepper
50g (2oz) butter
15-30ml (1-2 tbsp) lemon juice
5-10ml (1-2 tsp) capers, chopped
one egg yolk
90ml (6 tbsp) single cream

Divide the cod into four portions. Mix the flour, coriander and seasoning together. Coat the fish pieces with the seasoned flour. Melt the butter in a medium sauté pan and cook the fish gently until golden on both sides, turning once. Add 15ml (1 tbsp) lemon juice to the pan with the capers, cover tightly and continue cooking for a further 4-5 minutes, or until the fish is tender. Place the fish on a warmed serving dish. Mix the egg yolk and cream together, stir into the pan juices and heat gently until the sauce thickens slightly – do not boil. Adjust the seasoning, adding extra lemon juice if wished, and spoon the sauce over the fish. Serve immediately with creamed potatoes and green beans or Brussels sprouts.

MIXED GLAZED VEGETABLES
Serves 4

175g (6oz) carrots, peeled
175g (6oz) leeks, trimmed and washed
175g (6oz) celery, trimmed and washed
175g (6oz) cauliflower florets
225g (8oz) broccoli, trimmed, or 225g (8oz) frozen green beans
small piece of fresh root ginger, peeled
one 425g (15oz) can whole baby sweetcorn, drained
sesame oil
peanut oil
50g (2oz) demerara sugar
45ml (3 tbsp) lemon juice
salt and pepper

Thinly slice the carrots, leeks and celery diagonally. Split the cauliflower into small florets and cut the broccoli into small heads. Finely shred 5ml (1 tsp) root ginger. Halve the baby sweetcorn if large. Heat 15ml (1 tbsp) each of the oils in a large frying pan until smoky hot.

Add all the vegetables and half the ginger. Cook over a high heat, stirring, for 2-3 minutes, adding more oil if necessary. Stir in the sugar and lemon juice. Reduce the heat, cook, stirring for a further 3-4 minutes, until all the vegetables are just tender yet still crunchy. Season. Serve immediately with grilled bacon steaks or chicken.

HERRINGS IN OATMEAL WITH MUSTARD SAUCE
Serves 4

50g (2oz) butter
60ml (4 level tbsp) plain flour
salt and pepper
4 fresh herrings, filleted
one egg, beaten with 10ml (2 tsp) cold water
125g (4oz) medium oatmeal

Sauce

one 142ml (5floz) carton soured cream
25ml (1½ level tbsp) prepared English mustard

Butter an oven baking tray. Mix together flour and seasoning. Coat the herrings on both sides with the seasoned flour. Dip each into beaten egg, then coat evenly with the oatmeal. Arrange the herrings skin side down on the baking tray and dot them with the remaining butter. Bake in the oven for about 15 minutes, until well browned. Spoon the butter from the tray over the herrings and serve. For the sauce, mix together the soured cream, mustard, salt and pepper to taste. Serve the sauce separately.

Oven	Conventional	Fan
Temperature	220°C	200°C
Preheating	Recommended	Recommended
Shelf position	3rd	1st
Time	15-20 minutes	10-15 minutes

Herrings in Oatmeal with Mustard Sauce

Top: Spaghetti con Formaggio Bottom: Spanish Omelette

SPAGHETTI CON FORMAGGIO
Serves 2

150g (5oz) spaghetti	
225g (½lb) lean streaky bacon, rinded and chopped	
50g (2oz) onion, coarsely grated	
25g (1oz) butter	
125g (4oz) button mushrooms, sliced	
salt and pepper	
15ml (1 tbsp) salad oil	
175g (6oz) grated mature Cheddar cheese	
chopped parsley	

Cook the spaghetti in boiling salted water for 10 minutes. Put the chopped bacon in a frying pan and fry gently for 3 minutes, stirring occasionally with a wooden spoon. Add the onion and cook for a further 1 minute. Add the butter and sliced mushrooms, season lightly and cook for 4 minutes, stirring occasionally. Drain the pasta and return it to the pan with the salad oil. Using 2 forks, coat the spaghetti in the oil until it glistens. Heat the grill. Turn the spaghetti into a flameproof dish and spoon the bacon and mushroom mixture on top. Sprinkle with grated cheese and grill under a high heat for about 30 seconds. Sprinkle with chopped parsley before serving.

SPANISH OMELETTE
Serves 2

butter or oil for frying	
one small onion, chopped	
2-3 mushrooms, wiped and sliced	
one cooked potato, diced	
1 cap canned pimento (sweet red pepper), chopped	
small quantity cooked peas, beans or carrots	
4 eggs	
salt and pepper	
chopped parsley to garnish	

Put enough butter or oil in a 20.5cm (8 inch) frying pan just to cover the base. Add the onion and sauté until soft but not coloured. Add the mushrooms and cook until tender. Add the potato, pimento and cooked vegetables. Heat thoroughly. Lightly mix the eggs, season and pour over the vegetable mixture, which should be bubbling. When just set, turn upside down on to a heated serving dish. Garnish with chopped parsley and serve at once.

SAUTE OF TURKEY WITH PEAS
Serves 4

4 turkey joints, about 350g (12oz) each	
30ml (2 level tbsp) plain flour	
300ml (½ pint) chicken stock	
150ml (¼ pint) white wine	
15ml (1 tbsp) chopped fresh sage or 5ml (1 level tsp) dried	
salt and pepper	
450g (1lb) fresh peas, podded, or 225g (8oz) frozen	

Ease the skin and fat off the turkey joints, halve the leg joint. Snip the skin into small pieces. Place the skin in a large sauté pan and brown until crisp, reserve. Drain off all but 45ml (3 tbsp) fat from the sauté pan and brown the turkey joints. Sprinkle in the flour, stir to combine with fat and cook gently for 1 minute. Pour in the stock, wine, sage and seasoning and bring to the boil, cover the pan and simmer for 25 minutes, then turn the turkey pieces over. Add the peas to the pan, submerging them as much as possible. Cover and continue simmering for about 25 minutes, until the turkey and peas are tender. If using frozen peas, add them 5 minutes before the end of cooking time. Adjust the seasoning and garnish with crispy turkey skin.

STIR-FRIED SPINACH AND BEAN SPROUTS

Serves 4

450g (1lb) spinach or spring greens, trimmed and washed
peanut oil
50g (2oz) streaky bacon, rinded and thinly sliced
125g (4oz) frozen peas
225g (8oz) alfalfa sprouts
salt and pepper
150ml (¼ pint) natural yoghurt

Shred the spinach or spring greens very finely. Heat 30ml (2 tbsp) oil in a large frying pan until smoky hot. Stir in the spinach or greens, bacon and peas. Cook over a high heat for 3-4 minutes until the peas are tender, stirring all the time and adding a little more oil if necessary. Stir in the alfalfa sprouts. Cook for 1 minute to heat through. Season well and serve immediately drizzled with the yoghurt. Accompany with poached eggs and toast or bread.

SPICED CHICKEN WITH AVOCADO

Serves 4

350g (12oz) raw chicken breast without bone
30ml (2 level tbsp) plain flour
5ml (1 level tsp) cumin
5ml (1 level tsp) ground ginger
salt and pepper
30ml (2 tbsp) vegetable oil
one garlic clove, skinned and crushed
one 298g (10½oz) can bamboo shoots, thinly sliced
bunch of spring onions, trimmed and roughly chopped with green tops
one ripe avocado, stoned, peeled and thinly sliced
15ml (1 tbsp) lemon juice

Cut chicken into 1cm (½ inch) wide strips. Mix together the flour, cumin, ginger, salt and pepper. Coat the chicken with the seasoned flour. Heat the oil with garlic in a frying pan. When smoking, add the coated chicken pieces a few at a time, fry quickly until brown all over. Mix in the bamboo shoot slices and onion. Cook for about 1-2 minutes. Remove the pan from the heat, carefully stir in the avocado and lemon juice. Add more seasoning, if needed. Serve with boiled rice.

SPAGHETTI MILANESE

Serves 4

225g (8oz) spaghetti
grated Parmesan cheese

Sauce

½ onion, chopped
50g (2oz) mushrooms, chopped
25g (1oz) butter
225g (½lb) tomatoes, skinned and chopped, or 425g (15oz) can of tomatoes, drained
½ bayleaf
pinch dried thyme
pinch grated nutmeg
5ml (1 level tsp) sugar
salt and pepper
50g (2oz) ham, chopped
50g (2oz) tongue, chopped

Fry the onion and mushrooms in the butter for 3-5 minutes, until soft. Stir in the tomatoes, herbs and seasonings, cover and simmer gently for about 20 minutes, until the sauce has thickened and developed a good flavour. Add the ham and tongue and simmer uncovered for a further 5-10 minutes. Cook the spaghetti in fast-boiling, salted water in the usual way for 10-12 minutes until 'al dente' (to the bite), drain well and mix with the sauce on a heated dish. Serve the cheese in a separate dish.

PEANUT BASTED CHICKEN

Serves 4

4 chicken leg portions
75g (3oz) peanuts, roasted
140g (5½oz) butter or margarine
10ml (2 level tsp) ground cumin
salt and pepper
4 onion slices
4 small peaches, halved and stoned
chopped parsley to garnish

Divide each leg portion into two and remove the knobbly leg ends. Roughly chop half the nuts and grind the remainder in a blender. Beat all the nuts into 75g (3oz) of the fat with the cumin, salt and pepper. Line a grill pan with foil and arrange the chicken portions, skin-side down, in the pan. Spread a little of the nut mixture over the chicken, arrange the onion slices in the pan and dot with half the remaining fat. Grill gently for 10-15 minutes, roughing up the mixture on the portions with a fork from time to time to prevent burning. Turn the chicken over, spread with the remaining nut mixture, add the peach halves to the pan and dot with fat. Grill for a further 12-15 minutes until the chicken is tender. Serve the chicken topped with onion rings and parsley, with the grilled peach halves alongside.

Grill	
Temperature	250°C
Preheating	Recommended
Shelf position	2nd or 3rd
Time	25-30 minutes

Left: Spaghetti Milanese Above: Peanut Basted Chicken

Roasts

ROASTS

AUTOMATIC ROASTING

A special Miele oven feature is Automatic Roasting. A superb cooking system for all joints to be roasted using the fan oven. It will produce excellent results and at the same time seal and sear the meat, reducing shrinkage and spitting. The recommended cooking times allow for a slightly rare interior, (except for pork). If well roasted meat is preferred, allow an extra 15-20 minutes cooking time.

Pot Roasting is done at a lower temperature in a covered pot to retain steam which helps to moisten and tenderise tougher cuts of meat. The exterior can still be crisped by removing the pot lid before the end of the cooking time. Flavouring vegetables and herbs with liquid are included and these may be served as part of a gravy with the meat.

ROAST BEEF

Wipe the meat, trim if necessary then weigh and calculate the cooking time. Put the meat into the oven roasting tray using the anti-splash tray if liked, or on a rack over the tray, so that the thickest layer of fat is uppermost and the cut sides are exposed to the heat. Add about 50g (2oz) dripping or lard if the meat is lean. Cook the joint in the oven for the calculated time, basting from time to time with the juices from the tray. Serve accompanied by Yorkshire Pudding, horseradish sauce, thin brown gravy and vegetables as liked. Suitable joints for open roasting: sirloin, rib, rump, topside, aitch-bone. Very lean tender joints such as fillet may be roasted at a higher temperature 210°C conventional oven, 190°C fan oven allowing 8-10 minutes per 450g (1lb) meat.

Cooking times for Open Roast Beef		
Oven	**Conventional**	**Fan**
Temperature	200°C	180°C
Preheating	Recommended	Not necessary
Shelf position	2nd	1st
Time (according to weight of joint)	On the bone 20 minutes per 450g (1lb). For boned, rolled joints, add 5-10 minutes per 450g (1lb) to the cooking time	On the bone 15 minutes per 450g (1lb) Automatic roast can be used

Pot Roasted Beef. Suitable joints: are top rump (sometimes called thick flank), brisket, silverside, topside.

Cooking times for Pot Roast Beef		
Oven	**Conventional**	**Fan**
Temperature	190°C	160°C
Preheating	Recommended	Not necessary
Shelf position	1st	1st
Time (according to weight of joint)	30 minutes per 450g (1lb) plus 30 minutes	25 minutes per 450g (1lb) plus 25 minutes Automatic roast can be used

ROAST POTATOES

Cook in the oven tray for open roasting around the joint, basting several times during cooking. Allow about 1¼ hours in the conventional oven, for about 1 hour fan oven.

YORKSHIRE PUDDING

125g (4oz) plain flour

pinch of salt

one egg

300ml (½ pint) milk or two-thirds milk and one third water

Make up 300ml (½ pint) pouring batter. Put 25g (1oz) dripping or lard in a tin, heat on third shelf. When the fat in the tin shows a haze and is really hot, pour in the batter and return to the oven to cook for 40-45 minutes in the conventional oven, 30-35 minutes in the fan oven, until well risen, crisp and golden brown. **Note:** It is necessary to cook a batter in a tin to get a crisp puffed up result, cooked in a pie dish or flameproof ware, a batter tends to become soggy.

INDIVIDUAL PUDDINGS OR POPOVERS

50g (2oz) plain flour

a pinch of salt

one egg

150ml (¼ pint) milk

Make up the batter as for Yorkshire pudding. This quantity will fill a 4-cup Yorkshire pudding tin or, alternatively, 10-12 patty tins. Cook for about 15-20 minutes.

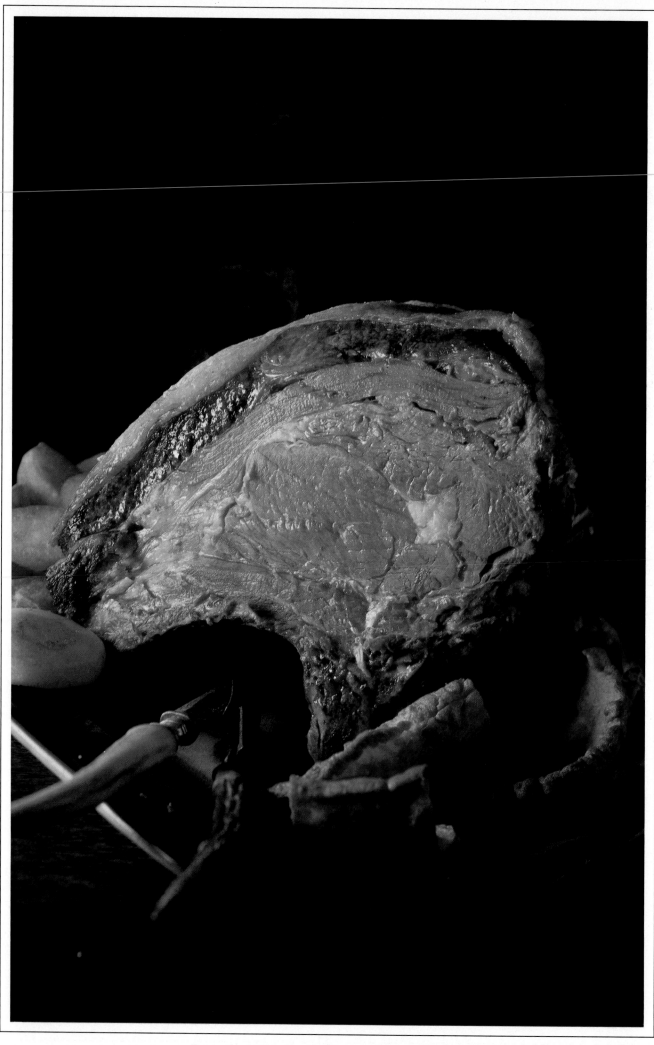

Roast Beef, Yorkshire Pudding and Roast Potatoes

Crown Roast of Lamb

ROASTS

BEEF POT ROAST BRISKET IN ALE

Serves 4

1¼kg (2½lb) joint lean brisket on the bone
30ml (2 tbsp) oil
2 onions, quartered
4 sticks celery, thickly sliced
2 parsnips, thickly sliced
salt and pepper
150ml (¼ pint) brown ale
150ml (¼ pint) beef stock

Heat the oil in a flameproof casserole and brown the beef on all sides. Pour any remaining oil from the casserole, arrange vegetables around the joint. Add salt, pepper, ale and stock, bring to the boil, cover and cook in the oven for the estimated cooking time until tender. Remove the lid for the last 20 minutes to brown the beef. Serve the meat with the vegetables and the liquid boiled to reduce to a syrup. Serve potatoes and extra vegetables with the meal.

Oven	Conventional	Fan
Temperature	190°C	160°C
Preheating	Recommended	Not necessary
Shelf position	1st	1st
Time	1¾ hours	1½ hours

ROASTED MINCED MEAT LOAF (Falscher Hase)

Serves 6

450g (1lb) minced beef
300g (11oz) minced pork
one large onion, finely chopped
50g (2oz) white bread, soaked in hot water and squeezed
one egg, beaten
10ml (2 level tsp) salt
5ml (1 level tsp) black pepper
5ml (1 level tsp) paprika
15ml (1 level tbsp) German mustard
5ml (1 level tsp) herbs, such as dried marjoram, oregano, sage (optional)
4 smoked streaky bacon rashers, rinded
7.5ml (1½ level tsp) cornflour
150ml (¼ pint) stock
60ml (4 tbsp) single cream

Mix together the minced beef, pork, onion, bread, egg, salt, pepper, paprika, mustard and herbs, if used. Mould the mixture into a loaf shape, put into a baking dish and lay bacon rashers on top. Cook in the oven for about 1¼ hours, until the meat is tender. Lift on to a serving dish and keep warm. Drain any excess fat from the dish. Blend the cornflour with the stock and stir with the cream into juices in the dish. Transfer to a pan and stir over the heat until boiling and thickened. Cut the loaf in slices, serve with the sauce, baked tomatoes and cauliflower.

Note: It is quite usual to combine different meats in a roast loaf such as fresh minced beef, lamb, pork, bacon, veal. Each meat contributes a special taste and texture to the finished dish. Various flavours can also be added with herbs and spices.

Oven	Conventional	Fan
Temperature	210°C	180°C
Preheating	Recommended	Not necessary
Shelf position	1st	1st
Time	1 hour 10-20 minutes	1 hour 20-30 minutes Automatic roast can be used

ROASTS

CROWN ROAST OF LAMB
Serves 6

| 2 pieces of best-end-of-neck, each with 6-7 cutlets |
| dripping if needed |
| cutlet frills |

Stuffing

| 50g (2oz) onion, finely chopped |
| 50g (2oz) celery, washed, trimmed and finely chopped |
| 225g (8oz) fresh breadcrumbs, toasted |
| one egg, lightly beaten |
| one garlic clove, skinned and crushed |
| 225g (8oz) cooked long-grain rice, about 75g (3oz) raw |
| 25g (1oz) butter |
| 10ml (2 level tsp) curry powder |
| salt and pepper |

If possible, the pieces of best end should be taken from opposite sides of the animal though this is not essential. They should be chopped, not chined, and sliced between the bones to about halfway down, the end of the bones being scraped clean. Trim neatly and bend round with the meaty side inwards to form a crown, securing it with skewers and string. Twist some pieces of foil round the exposed bones to prevent them burning. Mix together all the ingredients for the stuffing and insert into the centre of the prepared crown. Roast in the oven for the calculated cooking time, about 2 hours. Before serving, remove the foil and place small cutlet frills on the ends of the bones. **Variations:** Replace the above stuffing with sausage meat or sage and onion stuffing. Alternatively leave the centre unstuffed (fill with foil to keep the shape during the cooking) and spoon in cooked vegetables just before serving – diced carrots, peas or small potatoes garnished with parsley butter.

Oven	Conventional	Fan
Temperature	180°C	160°C
Preheating	Not necessary	Not necessary
Shelf position	1st	1st
Time (according to stuffed weight of joint)	30 minutes per 450g (1lb) plus 30 minutes	30 minutes per 450g (1lb) plus 30 minutes Automatic roast can be used

LAMB POT ROAST WITH GARLIC AND ROSEMARY
Serves 4

| 1.1-1.4kg (2½-3lb) half shoulder of lamb, boned |
| 3-4 garlic cloves, cut into slivers |
| salt and pepper |
| 30ml (2 tbsp) vegetable oil |
| 2 bacon rashers, rinded and chopped |
| one medium onion, thickly sliced |
| one medium carrot, peeled and thickly sliced |
| 2 sticks of celery, washed, trimmed and sliced |
| 75ml (5 tbsp) white wine |
| 150ml (¼ pint) stock |
| 1-2 rosemary sprigs |

Make slits into the lamb and insert the garlic slivers. Tie the joint in a neat shape, rub over with seasoning. In a flameproof casserole, heat the oil and fry the bacon for 1-2 minutes. Add all the vegetables and continue frying and stirring until the vegetables are lightly browned. Stir in the wine and when bubbling, mix in the stock and seasoning. Put the rosemary in the centre with the lamb on top. Cover and cook in the oven for the estimated cooking time until tender. Remove the lid for the last 20 minutes cooking time to brown the lamb. Lift out the meat, remove the string, keep warm. Strain the liquid and remove the fat with absorbent kitchen paper. Return the liquid to the casserole and boil to reduce to a syrup, thickened with a little cornflour if preferred. Serve the cooked vegetables if liked with the lamb.

Oven	Conventional	Fan
Temperature	180°C	160°C
Preheating	Not necessary	Not necessary
Shelf position	1st	1st
Time (according to weight of joint)	30 minutes per 450g (1lb) plus 30 minutes	25 minutes per 450g (1lb) plus 25 minutes Automatic roast can be used

ROASTS

ROLLED STUFFED BREAST OF LAMB

Serves 6

Joints containing a good percentage of bone can be boned (the butcher will usually do this), then rolled and tied into shape before being roasted in the usual way. If you wish, they can be stuffed before being rolled – this gives added flavour and helps to make the joints go further.

**one large boned breast of lamb,
about 1.6kg (3½ lb)**

salt and pepper

Veal Forcemeat

125g (4oz) fresh breadcrumbs

50g (2oz) shredded suet

15ml (1 level tbsp) chopped fresh parsley

grated rind of ½ lemon

salt and pepper

1 egg, beaten

Mix together the breadcrumbs, suet, parsley, lemon rind, seasoning and enough beaten egg to bind to a fairly firm mixture. Spread the boned out joint flat on a board, sprinkle with salt and pepper and rub the seasonings into the meat. Make up the veal forcemeat or any other suitable stuffing and spread this over the meat. Roll up the meat loosely, to allow the stuffing to expand during cooking. Tie in several places with fine string to hold it in shape. Place the meat on the rack over the roasting tin and cook in the oven for the calculated time, until well done. Remove the strings and serve sliced fairly thickly, accompanied by a thickened gravy. Any extra stuffing can be cooked in a separate small dish and served with the joint. Other cuts of lamb suitable for stuffing are shoulder and best-end-of-neck, they are cooked as for breast.

Oven	Conventional	Fan
Temperature	180°C	160°C
Preheating	Not necessary	Not necessary
Shelf position	2nd	1st
Time (according to weight of stuffed joint)	25 minutes per 450g (1lb) plus 25 minutes	25 minutes per 450g (1lb) plus 25 minutes Automatic roast can be used

ROAST LAMB

Serves 8

Lamb joints for roasting: Leg (whole or halved into shank and fillet), loin, best-end-of-neck also for Guard of Honour and Crown Roast, shoulder (whole or halved into blade and knuckle).

**one whole leg of lamb on the bone,
about 2.5kg (6lb)**

25g (1oz) dripping or lard or oil · salt & pepper

Wipe the meat, spread the skin with the fat and sprinkle with salt and pepper. Put the meat into the oven roasting pan using the anti-splash tray if liked or on a rack over the pan. Cook the joint in the oven for the calculated time, basting from time to time if liked. Add potatoes to roast if necessary about 1 hour before the end of cooking time. The lamb will be slightly pink in the centre when done, but will firm up while the rest of the meal is served. Serve accompanied by mint sauce or redcurrant jelly, new or roast potatoes, peas or green vegetable and a slightly thickened gravy.

Oven	Conventional	Fan
Temperature	200°C	180°C
Preheating	Not necessary	Not necessary
Shelf position	1st	1st
Time (according to weight of joint on the bone)	20 minutes per 450g (1lb) plus 20 minutes	15 minutes per 450g (1lb) plus 15 minutes Automatic roast can be used

For boned and rolled joints, add 5-10 minutes per 450g (1lb) to the cooking time.

LAMB EN CROUTE

Serves 10

1.6kg (3½ lb) leg of lamb, boned weight

150ml (¼ pint) red wine

450g (1lb) pork sausagemeat

125g (4oz) bacon rashers, rinded and chopped

salt and pepper · 25g (1oz) butter

225g (8oz) onions, sliced · one bay leaf

thyme sprig or a little dried thyme · 3 parsley stalks

one garlic clove, skinned and crushed

one 425g (15oz) can consommé or 450ml (¾ pint) stock made from lamb bones or stock cube

450g (1lb) ready-made puff pastry

beaten egg, to glaze · little flour · cornflour

braised celery heads and butter-glazed carrots, to garnish

Lamb en Croûte

Marinate the lamb in the wine for 2-3 hours, turning occasionally. Combine the sausagemeat, bacon and season well. Remove the meat from the wine and dry on absorbent kitchen paper. Stuff the cavity with the sausagemeat and sew up both ends with string. Melt the butter in a frying pan and fry the meat to seal the surface, then place in a casserole. Reheat the butter and fry the onions, add to the casserole with the thyme, bay leaf, parsley, garlic, marinade and consommé or stock. Cover and cook in the oven at the lower temperature. Take the meat from the casserole (reserving the juices) and allow to cool. Roll out the pastry into an oblong, 50 x 25cm (20 x 10 inch). Brush the meat surface with beaten egg and dust with flour. Place the lamb in the centre and make a parcel by folding the short ends over, sealing them with beaten egg; draw the long edges over and seal. Transfer to a baking tray, sealed side down. Decorate with the pastry trimmings and brush with beaten egg. Bake in the oven for about 35 minutes at the higher temperature, covering with foil if in danger of over-browning. Garnish with braised celery heads and carrots glazed with butter. To make the gravy, strain the juices from cooking the lamb and remove the fat with layers of absorbent kitchen paper. Thicken in the usual way with about 30ml (2 level tbsp) cornflour.

Oven	Conventional	Fan
Temperature	Lamb 170°C Pastry 210°C	Lamb 150°C Pastry 180°C
Preheating	Lamb not necessary Pastry recommended	Lamb not necessary Pastry recommended
Shelf position	1st	1st
Time	Lamb about 2 hours Pastry about 40-45 minutes	Lamb about 1¾ hours Pastry about 30-35 minutes Automatic roast can be used

CRUNCHY STUFFED PORK

Serves 4-6

| 1.4kg (3lb) lean joint belly pork with skin |
| lard, melted |

Stuffing

| 125g (4oz) soft white breadcrumbs |
| one onion, grated · grated rind of 1 lemon |
| ½ cooking apple, peeled, cored and grated |
| one stick of celery, washed and chopped |
| 2.5ml (½ level tsp) ground nutmeg |
| 40g (1½ oz) walnuts, chopped · salt and pepper |
| 25g (1oz) seedless raisins · 25g (1oz) butter, melted |
| one size 6 (small) egg, beaten |

Score the pork skin and remove the bones from the joint. To make the stuffing, mix the remaining ingredients and season to taste. Flatten the meat, skin side down and spread with the stuffing. Roll and secure with string tied around the joint. Weigh the joint to calculate cooking time. Rub salt generously into the skin and brush with a little melted lard. Roast in the oven for about 30 minutes to the 450g (1lb) and 30 minutes over, until the pork skin is crisp and brown. Carve in slices and serve hot or cold.

Oven	Conventional	Fan
Temperature	190°C	160°C
Preheating	Recommended	Not necessary
Shelf position	1st	1st
Time	2¼-2½ hours	2 hours
Automatic roast must be used		

ROAST PORK

Serves 6

Pork joints for roasting: Leg (whole or cut into fillet, knuckle or middle) loin, tenderloin, chump (generally boned). Trim the joint, then weigh and calculate the cooking time.

| 1½kg (3lb) joint leg fillet of pork |
| 15ml (1tbsp) oil · salt |

Rub the scored rind with the oil and salt to give crisp crackling. Put the joint into the oven roasting pan, using the anti-splash tray if liked or on a rack over the pan. Bake in the oven for the calculated time and serve well done (pork should never look pink when cooked), with apple or gooseberry sauce, sage and onion stuffing balls and baked dessert apple slices, and thickened gravy, roast potatoes, cauliflower and runner beans. Boned loin is particularly good stuffed with an apple and prune stuffing before roasting.

Oven	Conventional	Fan
Temperature	190°C	160°C
Preheating	Recommended	Not necessary
Shelf position	1st	1st
Time (according to weight of joint)	On the bone 20-25 minutes per 450g (1lb) plus 30 minutes; for boned and rolled joints add 5-10 minutes per 450g (1lb)	On the bone 25 minutes per 450g (1lb) plus 25 minutes Automatic roast can be used

VEAL IN PASTRY
(Kalbsbraten mit Kruste)

Serves 6-8

| 25g (1oz) butter or margarine |
| 1kg (2 lb) joint roasting veal, boned |
| salt and pepper |
| one small onion, chopped |
| 125g (4oz) mushrooms, wiped and thinly sliced |
| 5ml (1 level tsp) chopped fresh parsley |
| 2.5ml (½ level tsp) dried rosemary |
| one 368g (13 oz) packet frozen puff pastry, thawed |
| 1 egg, separated |

Heat some of the fat in a pan and brown the veal very thoroughly all over. Remove, sprinkle with salt and pepper and leave to cool. Add the remaining fat to the pan and fry the onion for a few minutes. Add the mushrooms and fry for 2-3 minutes. Remove the pan from the heat, stir in seasoning, the parsley and rosemary, leave to cool. Roll out the pastry to a rectangle large enough to enclose the joint. Spread the onion mixture evenly over the centre of the pastry and place the veal on top. Brush the pastry edges with egg white, fold carefully over the veal to make a neat parcel, sealing the pastry well with more egg white if necessary. Rinse the oven baking tray with water, put the wrapped veal on it, pastry join side down. Mix the egg yolk with 2.5ml (½ tsp) water and brush over the pastry. Add any pastry decorations and brush with egg. Cook in the oven for about 1½ hours, covering the joint with foil if it is browning too much.

Oven	Conventional	Fan
Temperature	220°C	200°C
Preheating	Recommended	Not necessary
Shelf position	2nd	2nd
Time	1 hour 20-30 minutes	1 hour 20-30 minutes Automatic roast can be used

Crunchy Stuffed Pork

ROASTS

POT ROAST VEAL
(Kalbsrahmbraten)

Serves 4

1kg (2 lb) joint roasting veal, boned
5ml (1 level tsp) salt
2.5ml (½ level tsp) white pepper
10ml (2 level tsp) paprika
50g (2oz) butter or margarine, softened
2 carrots, peeled and roughly chopped
2 onions, roughly chopped
2 tomatoes, quartered
2 veal bones (optional)
300ml (½ pint) single cream
15ml (1 level tbsp) cornflour
30ml (2 tbsp) water

Wipe the meat and season with the salt, pepper and paprika. Spread the butter over the meat and put into a casserole. Add the carrots, onions, tomatoes and bones, if used. Cover and cook in the oven for about 1 hour. Remove the lid, add half the cream and continue cooking for 45 minutes-1 hour until the veal is tender. Remove the veal to a serving dish and keep warm. Blend the cornflour with the water, stir into the casserole with the remaining cream and stir until boiled and thickened. Add a little extra water if the sauce seems too thick. Serve the veal and sauce accompanied with broccoli and pureéd potatoes.

Oven	Conventional	Fan
Temperature	210°C	170°C
Preheating	Recommended	Not necessary
Shelf position	1st	1st
Time	1¾-2 hours	1¾-2 hours Automatic roast can be used

SUGAR-GLAZED BAKED GAMMON

one gammon joint, about 1.4kg (3lb), soaked in cold water overnight
6 peppercorns · one bay leaf
onion stuck with a few cloves
30ml (2 tbsp) honey
45ml (2 level tbsp) soft brown sugar
some cloves

Garnish

2 oranges, 1 small onion, black olives

Drain the gammon and place in a large saucepan with the peppercorns, bay leaf and onion. Cover with cold water and bring to the boil, skimming the scum with a slotted draining spoon. Lower the heat and simmer gently for about 45 minutes or half the cooking time. Remove from the pan and allow to cool slightly. Cut off the rind and some of the fat. Score the remaining fat in a diamond pattern with a sharp knife, then brush with the honey mixed with the sugar, and stud the diamond shapes with cloves. Wrap in foil, place in roasting tin and bake in the oven for the rest of the cooking time. Unwrap the foil to expose the glazed fat only for the last 20 minutes of cooking time. Transfer to a warmed serving platter and garnish with orange twists and slices, thinly sliced onion and black olives as shown in the picture.

Oven	Conventional	Fan
Temperature	180°C	150°C
Preheating	Recommended	Not necessary
Shelf position	2nd	1st
Time (according to weight of joint)	20 minutes per 450g (1lb) plus 20 minutes	20 minutes per 450g (1lb) plus 20 minutes Automatic roast can be used

CHICKEN WITH LEMON SAUCE

Serves 4-6

1.8kg (4lb) oven ready chicken with giblets
165(5½ oz) softened butter
salt and pepper
15ml (1 tbsp) lemon juice
10ml (2 level tsp) dried tarragon
1 lemon, quartered

Sauce

50g (2oz) butter
15ml (1 level tbsp) plain flour
150ml (¼ pint) stock, made with the giblets
15ml (1 tbsp) lemon juice
150ml (¼ pint) double cream

Make stock with the giblets then boil to reduce it down to 150ml (¼ pint) to give a concentrated flavour. Prepare the chicken for roasting by mixing 75g (3oz) of the butter with 1.25ml (¼ level tsp) salt, some freshly ground pepper and 10ml (2 tsp) of the lemon juice. Add the tarragon, then put half this mixture inside the chicken and spread the remainder evenly all over the outside. Place lemon quarters inside the chicken. Place the chicken in a roasting tin and cover the breast with buttered foil. Bake in the oven for about 1½ hours, basting the chicken frequently with the buttery juices, until the chicken is cooked – when a fine skewer is pierced into the thigh and no pink juices run out. Remove the foil from the breast during the last 30 minutes. Remove the chicken to a serving dish and keep warm. For the sauce, melt the butter in a small saucepan, stir in the flour and cook for 1 minute. Gradually stir in the chicken stock and lemon juice. Bring to the boil, stirring all the time and simmer for 2-3 minutes. Add the cream and some of the chicken juices from the roasting tin. Carve the chicken and serve on a bed of rice with the sauce poured over.

Oven	Conventional	Fan
Temperature	200°C	170°C
Preheating	Recommended	Not necessary
Shelf position	1st	1st
Time	About 1½ hours	About 1½ hours Automatic roast can be used

ROAST CHICKEN

Serves 6

one chicken with giblets 1.6kg (3½lb)
50g (2oz) butter, softened
salt and pepper
3-4 rashers streaky bacon, rinded
15ml (1 level tbsp) flour
300ml (½ pint) giblet stock

If the bird is frozen, allow it to thaw out completely, then remove the bag of giblets. Wash the inside of the bird and stuff it at the neck end before folding the neck skin over. To add flavour you can put an onion, a thick lemon wedge or a knob of butter in the body of the bird. Spread the chicken with the butter or oil and sprinkle with salt and pepper. Put in the roasting tin. A few strips of streaky bacon may be laid over the breast to prevent it from becoming too dry. Bake in the oven basting from time to time if not on the rotisserie. Put a piece of paper over the breast if the flesh shows signs of becoming too brown. Alternatively, wrap the chicken in foil before roasting; allow the same cooking time, but open the foil for the final 15-20 minutes, to allow the bird to brown. Serve with roast potatoes and a green vegetable or, for a change, a tossed green salad. Bacon rolls, forcemeat balls, small chipolata sausages, bread sauce and gravy are the usual accompaniments.

The gravy, pour off all the fat except 15ml (1 tbsp) from the roasting tin. Sprinkle in 15ml (1 level tbsp) flour and stir in about 300ml (½ pint) giblet stock. Bring to the boil, stirring, season with salt and pepper and add a touch of

gravy browning if necessary. The finely chopped chicken liver may be included to give a richer flavour.

Oven	Conventional	Fan
Temperature	200°C	160°C
Preheating	Recommended	Not necessary
Shelf position	2nd	2nd
Time (according to dressed weight of chicken)	20 minutes per 450g (1lb) plus 20 minutes. Using the rotisserie for a 1.4kg (3lb) chicken allow about 1¼ hours	20 minutes per 450g (1lb) plus 20 minutes Automatic roast can be used

ROAST GOOSE (Gans)

Serves 6

one goose, about 4kg (8½lb)
salt
15ml (1 level tbsp) cornflour
one 142ml (5 floz) carton soured cream

Remove the giblets and wipe the goose inside and out. Prick the skin gently without piercing the meat to allow fat to escape. Season with salt inside and out. Lay the bird breast side down on the anti-splash tray in the roasting pan. Roast in the oven for about 1 hour, then turn the goose over and baste. Continue cooking, basting several times until the bird is tender – when a fine skewer is pierced into the thigh no pink juices run out. Remove the goose to a serving dish and keep warm. Drain off excess fat from the tray, blend the cornflour into the remaining juices, add the soured cream and stir until boiling and thickened. Serve the goose and sauce accompanied with roast potatoes, brussels sprouts and apple sauce. If liked the goose may be stuffed with cooking apples, cut into pieces, or with a stuffing made with the gizzard, heart, liver, breadcrumbs, seasoning, nutmeg and egg.

Oven	Conventional	Fan
Temperature	190°C	160°C
Preheating	Recommended	Not necessary
Shelf position	1st	1st
Time	3 hours	2¾-3 hours Automatic roast can be used

Sugar-Glazed Baked Gammon

Roast Turkey with Chestnut Stuffing

ROAST TURKEY
WITH CHESTNUT STUFFING

To serve 13-15

4.5-5.9kg (10-13lb) oven-ready turkey

To serve 20-30

7.3-9kg (16-20lb) oven-ready turkey

An oven-ready turkey of 4kg (9lb) is equivalent to one of 5.4kg (12lb) undressed weight. It is usual to stuff the neck end of the turkey with veal forcemeat or chestnut stuffing; allow 450g (1lb) made stuffing for a bird of up to 6.3kg (14lb); twice this amount for a larger bird. For the body cavity, a savoury breadcrumb stuffing is generally used – allow 450-900g (1-2lb) according to size. Make the turkey as plump and even in shape as possible, then truss it with the wings folded under the body and the legs tied together. Weigh the stuffed bird to calculate cooking time. Before cooking the bird, spread it with softened dripping or butter; the breast may also be covered with strips of fat bacon. If you are going to roast by the quick method, it is best to wrap the bird in foil to prevent the flesh drying and the skin hardening. Foil is not recommended for the slow method of cooking, as it tends to give a steamed rather than a roasted bird. In the conventional oven, for the slow method, roast at 170°C; for the quick method, 230°C, calculating the time according to the chart. In the fan oven roast at 160°C. Calculate to be ready 30 minutes before serving. To test if done, pierce the thigh flesh with a skewer and juices should run clear with no hint of pink. If the turkey is cooked, lower the heat and keep the bird hot. If not, continue cooking. Unless the bird is cooked in foil, baste regularly, turning round once to ensure even browning. Foil, if used, should be unwrapped for the last 30 minutes, so that the bird may be well basted and then left to become crisp and golden. Garnish and accompaniments; small sausages, forcemeat balls, rolls of bacon and watercress. Serve with brown gravy and bread sauce. Cranberry or some other sharp sauce can also be served. Sliced tongue or ham is a favourite accompaniment.

Frozen Turkeys: It is important that turkeys and all frozen poultry are thawed completely. Thawing at room temperature is best then birds should be refrigerated if not cooked immediately.

Guide Thawing Times			
oven-ready	takes about	oven-ready	takes about
1.4kg (3lb)	9 hours	6.8kg (15lb)	24 hours
2.3kg (5lb)	15 hours	9kg (20lb)	30 hours
4.5kg (10lb)	18 hours		

Cooking Times Conventional Oven		
	Quick method	Slow method
Temperature	230°C	170°C
Preheating	Not necessary	Not necessary
Shelf position	1st	1st
Weight	Time	Time
2.7-3.6kg (6-8lb)	2¼-2½ hours	3-3½ hours
3.6-4.5kg (8-10lb)	2½-2¾ hours	3½-3¾ hours
4.5-5.4kg (10-12lb)	2¾ hours	3¼-4 hours
5.4-6.3kg (12-14lb)	3 hours	4-4¼ hours
6.3-7.3kg (14-16lb)	3-3¼ hours	4¼-4½ hours
7.3-8.2kg (16-18lb)	3¼-3½ hours	4½-4¾ hours
9-10kg (20-22lb)	3½-3¾ hours	4¾-5 hours

Cooking Times Fan Oven	
Temperature	160°C
Preheating	Use Automatic roast
Shelf position	1st
Time	Turkeys up to 5.4kg (12lb) allow 15 minutes per 450g (1lb) stuffed weight Turkeys up to 9kg (20lb) allow 10 minutes per 450g (1lb) stuffed weight

CHESTNUT STUFFING

50g (2oz) bacon, rinded and chopped

125g (4oz) fresh breadcrumbs

5ml (1 tsp) chopped fresh parsley

25g (1oz) butter, melted · grated rind of 1 lemon

225g (8oz) chestnut pureé (see note)

salt and pepper · one egg, beaten

Fry the bacon gently in its own fat for about 3-5 minutes until crisp. Drain and add the rest of the ingredients, binding with the beaten egg. This stuffing is suitable for a 4.5kg (10lb) turkey.

Note: Chestnut pureé may be made from fresh, dried or canned chestnuts, or use canned unsweetened pureé. To peel fresh chestnuts, snip the brown outer skins with a pair of scissors or sharp knife and place the chestnuts in a pan of boiling water for 3-5 minutes. Lift out a few at a time and peel off both the brown and inner skins. To cook, simmer gently in a little chicken stock for about 35-40 minutes until tender. 450g (1lb) fresh chestnuts gives 350g (12oz) peeled, and when cooked as above and then pureéd yields about 400g (14oz) unsweetened pureé. Whole canned, unsweetened – use as fresh cooked chestnuts. Canned pureé, unsweetened – use as fresh cooked pureé.

Dried Chestnuts: Reconstituted, dried chestnuts can be used as fresh cooked chestnuts. To prepare, soak overnight in cold water, then simmer in stock or milk until tender – about 40 minutes. 450g (1lb) dried chestnuts gives 900g (2lb) whole chestnuts.

ROAST DUCKLING JAPANESE-STYLE (Japanische Ente)
Serves 6

one duckling, about 1.8kg (4lb) and giblets
300ml (½ pint) water · salt

Stuffing	75g (3oz) ground almonds

one banana, peeled & mashed · 60g (2½oz) raisins
one garlic clove, skinned and crushed
2.5ml (½ level tsp) black pepper · 2 eggs, beaten
2.5ml (½ level tsp) curry powder
30ml (2 tbsp) port · one onion, chopped
125g (4oz) fresh brown breadcrumbs

Sauce	15ml (1 level tbsp) cornflour

one 142ml (5floz) carton soured cream
one 225g (8oz) can pineapple slices, drained and diced
2 fresh or canned apricots, halved and stoned
50g (2oz) morello cherries, stoned, cooked or canned
50g (2oz) mandarin segments, fresh or canned
2 bananas, peeled and sliced
2 dessert apples, peeled, cored and chopped

Clean the duckling inside and out. Rub with salt. Cook the giblets in the water with salt for about 20 minutes until tender. Drain and finely dice the heart, liver and gizzard. Retain the cooking liquid for the sauce. For the stuffing, mix together the almonds, banana, raisins, onion, garlic, pepper, egg, curry powder, port, breadcrumbs, and salt to make a soft mixture. Spoon into the duckling cavity. Secure with skewers and put the duckling breast side down in a roasting tin and add about 150ml (¼ pint) water. Roast in the oven for about 1 hour, then turn the duckling over and baste. Continue cooking, basting several times until the bird is tender – when a fine skewer is pierced into the thigh no pink juices run out. Remove the duckling and keep warm. For the sauce, drain the fat from the roasting tin, stir the giblet liquid into the pan juices then pour into a pan. Blend the cornflour with the liquid, add the soured cream and stir over the heat until boiling and thickened. Add the fruits and heat through. Carve the duckling and serve with the stuffing and sauce accompanied with roast potatoes, peas and seasonal green vegetables.

Oven	Conventional	Fan
Temperature	200°C	160°C
Preheating	Recommended	Not necessary
Shelf position	1st	1st
Time	2-2½ hours	2-2½ hours Automatic roast can be used

ROAST DUCKLING WITH APRICOT STUFFING
Serves 4

one oven ready duckling, about 2-2.5kg (4-5lb)
25g (1oz) butter, melted
salt and pepper
30ml (2 tbsp) warmed honey

Stuffing
125g (4oz) long-grain rice, cooked and drained
125g (4oz) dried apricots, soaked overnight, drained and chopped
50g (2oz) almonds or hazelnuts, chopped
50g (2oz) currants or raisins
45ml (3 tbsp) chopped fresh parsley
one egg, beaten

To garnish
8 canned apricot halves, drained
knob of butter

Wash the duckling and dry thoroughly with absorbent kitchen paper. Use the duckling giblets for stock to make gravy with juices from the roasting tin. To prepare the stuffing, put all the ingredients in a mixing bowl and season to taste, binding the mixture with the beaten egg. Place the duckling on a board and fill the cavity with the stuffing, reserving 45ml (3 level tbsp) for the garnish. Tie or sew with trussing string, securing with skewers if necessary. Brush with the butter, sprinkle liberally with salt and pepper and coat with the honey. Prick all over with a fork and place on the rack in the roasting tin. Roast in the oven for about 2 hours, until the duckling is tender when pierced with a skewer and well browned. Baste with juices during cooking. Fifteen minutes before the end of cooking time, put 5ml (1 tsp) of the reserved stuffing into each apricot half. Dot each with a little butter and put in a greased ovenproof dish or on a baking tray. Put in the oven to heat through. Remove the duckling from the rack and discard the trussing string, and skewers if used. Transfer to a warmed serving platter and garnish with the stuffed apricot halves.

Oven	Conventional	Fan
Temperature	200°C	160°C
Preheating	Recommended	Not necessary
Shelf position	2nd	1st
Time	About 2 hours	2-2½ hours Automatic roast can be used

Cream of Lemon Soup, Lamb with Almonds a

...smati Rice, Apple and Mint Relish, Spinach Salad

SPRING DINNER PARTY

MENU FOR SIX

CREAM OF LEMON SOUP

A rich, jellied homemade chicken stock is by far the best for this soup.

25g (1oz) butter
175g (6oz) onion, thinly sliced
75g (3oz) carrot, peeled and thinly sliced
75g (3oz) celery, washed, trimmed and thinly sliced
2 lemons
1.1 litre (2 pint) chicken stock
2 bay leaves
salt and pepper
150ml (¼ pint) milk
snipped chives, to garnish

Melt the butter in a large saucepan and add the vegetables. Cover the pan and cook gently for 10-15 minutes, until the vegetables are beginning to soften. Meanwhile, thinly pare the lemons using a potato peeler. Blanch the rinds in boiling water for 1 minute, drain. Squeeze the juice from the lemons to give 75-90ml (5-6 tbsp). Add the lemon rind and juice to the pan with the stock, bay leaves and seasoning. Bring slowly to the boil, cover and simmer gently for about 40 minutes, until the vegetables are very soft. Cool the soup a little, remove the bay leaves. Purée the vegetable and lemon mixture in blender until quite smooth. Return the soup to a clean pan, reheat gently, stirring in the milk. Do not boil. Adjust the seasoning and serve garnished with snipped chives.

LAMB WITH ALMONDS

If you use lamb shoulder instead of leg, buy one weighing about 2.5kg (5½lb) to allow for wastage when trimming. You need about 1.1kg (2½lb) lean meat.

2kg (4½lb) leg of lamb on the bone
60ml (4 tbsp) vegetable oil
225g (8oz) onion, finely chopped
15ml (1 level tbsp) ground ginger
5ml (1 level tsp) paprika
75g (3oz) ground almonds
90ml (3fl oz) light stock
300ml (½ pint) single cream
1 garlic clove, skinned and crushed
salt and pepper
25g (1oz) fresh root ginger, peeled and finely chopped
chopped fresh parsley, to garnish

Remove the meat from the bone and cut into 2.5cm (1 inch) pieces, discarding skin and fat. Heat the oil in a medium flameproof casserole and brown the meat a little at a time. Remove from the pan using a slotted draining spoon. Add the onion to the casserole and sprinkle over the ground ginger and paprika. Cook gently for 1 minute, stirring. Mix in the ground almonds, stock, cream, garlic and seasoning, then bring to the boil. Replace the meat, stir well and cover tightly. Cook in the oven, 170°C conventional oven/150°C fan oven/1st shelf, for about 1¼ hours. Stir the root ginger into the casserole, cover and return to the oven for a further 20 minutes, until the meat is quite tender. Skim well, adjust the seasoning and spoon into a warmed serving dish. Cover and keep warm. Garnish with parsley.

APPLE AND MINT RELISH

Fresh mint gives much better results than dried.

275g (10oz) cooking apples, peeled and cored
150ml (¼ pint) natural yoghurt
30ml (2 tbsp) chopped fresh mint
salt and pepper

Coarsely grate the apples and stir into the yoghurt with the mint and seasoning. Spoon into a serving dish, cover with cling film and refrigerate until serving time. Garnish with a sprig of mint.

BASMATI RICE

350g (12oz) Basmati rice

Boil in plenty of salted water for about 12 minutes until just tender. Drain well. Arrange around the lamb to serve.

SPINACH SALAD

Use tender, young leaves. Instead of sesame seeds you can scatter over roughly chopped or crushed plain roasted, not salted, peanuts.

450g (1lb) leaf spinach, washed and trimmed
8 spring onions
5ml (1 level tsp) Dijon mustard
90ml (6 tbsp) vegetable oil
30ml (2 tbsp) wine vinegar
salt and pepper
40g (1½oz) toasted sesame seeds

Roughly shred the spinach and place in a large salad bowl. Snip the spring onions over the spinach, cover with cling film and refrigerate. In a lidded jar, shake the mustard, oil, vinegar and seasoning together. Just before serving, toss the spinach in the dressing. Sprinkle over the sesame seeds.

RHUBARB ICE CREAM

The smooth texture of this ice is a cross between a sorbet and a custard cream.

700g (1½lb) pink rhubarb, trimmed
60ml (4 level tbsp) redcurrant jelly
90ml (6 tbsp) water
one 397g (14oz) can condensed milk, chilled
150ml (¼ pint) natural yoghurt

Slice the rhubarb into 2.5cm (1 inch) lengths and place in a medium saucepan. Add the redcurrant jelly and water, then cover the pan tightly. Simmer gently until the rhubarb is soft and pulpy. Purée the rhubarb mixture in a blender until really smooth. Pour into a large bowl, cool. Stir the chilled condensed milk and yoghurt into the rhubarb mixture until evenly blended. Pour the mixture into a freezer container to give a depth of about 6.5cm (2½ inches) – do not use a metal dish. Freeze the mixture until firm, then overwrap and return to the freezer until required. Leave the ice cream at a cool room temperature for 20-30 minutes before serving to allow it to soften slightly. Scoop into individual dishes. Serve with Walnut Shorties.

WALNUT SHORTIES

Light soft brown sugar makes a pleasant variation.

75g (3oz) butter, softened
50g (2oz) caster sugar
125g (4oz) self raising flour
.5ml (1 level tsp) ground cinnamon
one egg yolk · 12 walnut halves

Beat the butter until light and creamy. Gradually work in the sugar keeping the mixture light. Sift the flour and cinnamon over the creamed ingredients, add the egg yolk and stir together until evenly mixed. Knead lightly until just smooth. Roll the dough into twelve even-sized balls and place well apart on the oven baking tray. Place a walnut half on each one. Bake in the oven, 180°C conventional oven/160°C fan oven/4th shelf, for about 12 minutes, until lightly browned. Allow to cool on the tray for a few minutes, then ease off and complete cooling on a wire rack. Store in an airtight container.

COUNTDOWN

The day before: Prepare the ice cream and freeze. Bake the Walnut Shorties, cool, then store in an airtight container.
The morning: Prepare the soup, cook and purée, don't reheat or add milk yet. Cut up the lamb, refrigerate loosely covered. Skin and finely chop the onion, refrigerate tightly covered. Wash and dry some parsley sprigs, store in a polythene bag in the refrigerator. Prepare the spinach and spring onions, place in a salad bowl; cover tightly with cling film and refrigerate. Prepare the dressing but don't add to the salad yet. Toast the sesame seeds, cool, store in an airtight container. Make the apple and mint relish, refrigerate tightly covered. Boil Basmati rice until tender – drain well. Place in a well-buttered shallow ovenproof dish, season, cover. Store in a cool place.
To serve at 8pm:
6pm: Brown the meat and complete the lamb dish, put in the oven to cook. Open and decant the claret.
About 7.15pm: Put the rice in the oven to reheat. Peel and chop the root ginger, add to the lamb dish, re-cover and return to the oven.
7.45pm: Check the lamb and rice. Reheat the soup and add the milk – do not boil.
Around 8pm: Serve the meal. Garnish the soup with snipped chives. Toss the Spinach Salad with the dressing before serving. Leave the ice cream at a cool room temperature for 20-30 minutes before scooping.
To accompany the lamb, we suggest a fine claret, such as the Château La Lagune 1978, as good as you can afford, or an equivalent type wine from say Spain or America.

Hot Veal and Ham Terrine, Vichy Carrots, Potatoes ▸

rlic, *Fresh Apricot Shortcake with Crème Anglaise*

SUMMER DINNER PARTY

SPICED ONIONS

Large onions could be used when shallots or button onions are unobtainable. Skin the onions, cut them into quarters or eighths, keeping the root ends intact to prevent the onions falling apart.

700g (1½lb) small shallots or button onions, skinned
25g (1oz) butter
15ml (1 level tbsp) ground cumin
one large green pepper, halved, deseeded and diced
one 225g (8oz) can tomatoes
15ml (1 tbsp) cider vinegar
12 black olives, halved and stoned
salt and pepper
watercress, to garnish

Skin the shallots or button onions. This is made easier by covering the onions in boiling water and leaving them to stand for 2-3 minutes; the skins will peel away quite easily. Melt the butter in a medium saucepan and gently fry the cumin for 1-2 minutes. Add the onions and pepper. Cook, stirring for a few minutes before adding the tomatoes, vinegar and olives. Simmer very gently for at least 10 minutes, until the onions and pepper are cooked. Season, pour into a bowl and leave to cool. Cover and chill well before serving in individual dishes. Garnish with watercress and serve with melba toast.

MELBA TOAST

Can be made in advance and keeps crisp for up to a week if stored in an airtight container.

6 slices of medium cut white bread

Toast the bread on 4th runner, grill setting 275°C. Remove the crusts, then insert a sharp knife into each slice and cut through to form two slices. Cut each split slice into two triangles. Return with the untoasted side uppermost to the grill until lightly browned and crisped. When cold, pack carefully in an airtight container.

HOT VEAL AND HAM TERRINE

An interesting combination of flavours; don't be alarmed that the centre remains pink, it's because of the layer of ham.

700g (1½lb) minced veal
2 size 1 or 2 (large) eggs
300ml (½ pint) single cream
salt and pepper
1.25ml (¼ level tsp) ground nutmeg
30ml (2 tbsp) dry sherry
40g (1½oz) butter
one bunch watercress, washed, trimmed and finely chopped
one garlic clove, skinned and crushed
125g (4oz) button mushrooms, wiped and finely sliced
125g (4oz) sliced cooked ham
one bay leaf
5ml (1 level tsp) arrowroot

In a blender, purée together the veal, eggs, cream, 2.5ml (½ level tsp) salt, pepper, nutmeg and sherry. This will probably have to be done in two batches. Melt half the butter in a frying pan and sauté the watercress and garlic for about 2-3 minutes until softened. Set aside to cool. In the same pan, melt the remaining butter and sauté the mushrooms until just cooked. Set aside to cool. Cut one slice of ham into fine shreds, cover and reserve. Cut the remaining ham into wide strips and put with the mushrooms. Base line an ovenproof 1.4 litre (2½ pint) terrine dish with greaseproof paper. Divide the veal mixture into three. Place alternate layers of veal, watercress, ham and mushrooms in the prepared dish, beginning and ending with a layer of veal. Place the bay leaf on top. Cover tightly with foil. Place in a roasting tin (bain marie) and pour in sufficient hot water to come half way up the sides of the terrine. Cook in the oven, 180°C conventional oven/160°C fan oven/1st shelf, for about 1¼-1½ hours, until just firm to the touch. When cooked, drain the juices into a saucepan through a sieve lined with muslin. Turn the terrine on to a serving dish and gently scrape away the creamy curd from the sides. Rub this through the strainer and add to the juices. Cover the terrine and keep warm in a slow oven. Bring the juices to the boil, stir in the arrowroot mixed to a smooth paste with a little water. Simmer, whisking all the time until slightly thickened. Adjust seasoning. Add the reserved shreds of ham and spoon over the terrine.

VICHY CARROTS

An attractive way to serve carrots and still retain their crispness.

900g (2lb) carrots, peeled · salt and pepper
90ml (6 tbsp) light stock · 25g (1oz) butter
chopped fresh parsley, to garnish

Cut the carrots into fine matchsticks. Place in a large saucepan of boiling salted water. Bring back to the boil and boil for 1 minute. Drain in a colander or sieve. Place the carrots under running cold water to stop them cooking further. Put in to a deep 1.1 litre (2 pint) ovenproof dish. Pour in the stock and dot the butter on top of the carrots. Season and cover tightly. Cook in the oven, 180°C conventional oven/160°C fan oven/3rd shelf, for about 30-40 minutes, until tender. Stir once during the cooking time. Adjust the seasoning before serving. Garnish with parsley.

POTATOES WITH GARLIC

900g (2lb) small new potatoes, scrubbed · salt
50g (2oz) butter · 2 garlic cloves, skinned & crushed

Place the potatoes in a saucepan of salted water, cover and cook until just tender. Drain well. Clean the pan, add and melt the butter. Mix in the garlic, toss in potatoes to glaze with butter.

FRESH APRICOT SHORTCAKE

If ripe apricots are unavailable, use well drained canned or cooked dried apricots.

150g (5oz) butter, softened
50g (2oz) soft dark brown sugar
175g (6oz) self raising flour · 25g (1oz) ground rice
grated rind of 1 lemon · 15g (½oz) caster sugar
450g (1lb) fresh apricots, quartered and stoned
125g (4oz) full fat soft cheese · one egg
almond essence · 15g (½oz) flaked almonds

Lightly grease a 20.5cm (8 inch) loose-based metal flan tin. In a mixing bowl, beat the butter and sugar together until soft and fluffy. Mix in the flour, ground rice and lemon rind until the mixture forms a dough. Press into the prepared tin with floured fingertips. Prick well with a fork. Bake in the oven, 190°C conventional oven/170°C fan oven/3rd shelf, for about 25-35 minutes, until light browned and cooked through. Arrange the apricots on the shortcake base. Sprinkle the caster sugar over them. Beat together the soft cheese, egg and almond essence to taste until smooth. Spoon over the apricots, covering completely both the fruit and shortcake. Scatter over the flaked almonds. Bake in the oven, 180°C conventional oven/160°C fan oven/3rd or 4th shelf, for about 35-45 minutes, until golden. Ease out of the tin and serve warm or cold with Crème Anglaise.

CREME ANGLAISE

2 eggs · 5ml (1 level tsp) caster sugar
300ml (½ pint) milk · pared rind of 1 lemon

Whisk the eggs and sugar lightly. Scald the milk and lemon rind, then strain on to the egg mixture. Return to a clean pan and stir over low hob heat, or use a double saucepan, and stir until the sauce thickens and lightly coats the back of the wooden spoon. Do not allow to boil. Serve warm.

COUNTDOWN

The day before: Prepare the Spiced Onions. Cool, cover with cling film and keep refrigerated. Make the Melba Toast, store in an airtight container until required. Prepare and bake the base of the Fresh Apricot Shortcake. Cool, then foil wrap and store in a cool place. Beat together the cream cheese, egg and almond essence. Cover and keep refrigerated.

The morning: Prepare the ingredients for the Veal and Ham Terrine and layer into the dish. Cover and keep refrigerated. Refrigerate the shreds of ham in a polythene bag. Wash watercress for garnish, and refrigerate in a polythene bag. Prepare the carrots, blanch, drain well then spoon into the cooking dish. Don't add the stock yet, cover and refrigerate. Clean the potatoes, dry and store in a cool place. Make the Crème Anglaise, cover with damp grease-proof paper, and refrigerate.

To serve at 8pm:

About 6pm: Preheat the oven.

6.15pm: Stand the prepared terrine in the roasting tin half filled with water and put into oven to cook. Stir the Spiced Onions and spoon into individual serving dishes. Keep refrigerated. Garnish with watercress before serving.

7pm: Prepare the apricots and arrange on shortcake. Spoon the cream cheese mixture evenly over and scatter with almonds. Place in the oven to cook. When cooked, leave at room temperature.

7.15pm: Add stock, butter and seasoning to carrots. Place in oven below terrine.

7.30pm: Boil the potatoes until tender, toss in the garlic and butter with seasoning. Cover and keep warm in a slow oven.

7.45pm: Drain juices from terrine into saucepan. Turn oven down to low. Turn the terrine on to serving dish and strain the creamy curds into juices. Cover terrine and keep warm in oven. Thicken the juices, adjust seasoning. Stir in shreds of ham. Keep sauce warm over a low heat. Place Crème Anglaise over pan of simmering water to warm.

8pm: Serve the meal. Serve the wine cool and fresh, but not chilled.

To accompany the Terrine, we suggest a rosé, in this case a 1983 Rosenmuskateller from Italy, or a red, such as Mercurey, Dão or Zinfandel.

Savoury Eggs with Stilton, Veal Escalopes with Cucumber, Butt

...nge-Tout, Frozen Meringue Cream with Spiced Red Plums

MENU FOR SIX

SAVOURY EGGS WITH STILTON

Danish Mycella makes a very pleasant alternative to Stilton.

6 eggs
50g (2oz) butter, softened
125g (4oz) Stilton cheese, crumbled
45ml (3 tbsp) single cream
50g (2oz) walnut pieces
2 sticks of celery heart, finely chopped
salt and pepper
celery leaves to garnish

Hard-boil the eggs and leave in the saucepan with cold water running over them until quite cold. Quick cooling helps to prevent a grey line appearing between the yolk and white. Meanwhile beat the butter until quite smooth and gradually work in the cheese and single cream. Shell and halve the eggs lengthways. Sieve the yolks into the cheese mixture. Place the whites in a bowl of cold water until required. Finely chop half the walnuts and beat into the cheese mixture with the celery; season to taste. Spoon into a piping bag fitted with a 1cm (½ inch) plain nozzle. Pat the egg whites dry with absorbent kitchen paper and pipe the cheese filling into the centre of each. Place side-by-side in a shallow-rimmed serving dish and garnish with remaining walnut pieces. Cover with cling film and chill well. Take out of the refrigerator 30 minutes before serving. Fill the centre with celery leaves and serve with French bread or rolls.

VEAL ESCALOPES WITH CUCUMBER

To give more depth of flavour to the wine for cooking, start with 300ml (½ pint) and boil to reduce by half in an open pan. Take care too when browning the veal. Chicken can be used as an alternative to veal.

½ cucumber, peeled
6 veal escalopes, about 75g (3oz) each
salt and pepper
25g (1oz) butter
30ml (2 tbsp) corn oil
125g (4oz) onion, sliced
one garlic clove, skinned and crushed
150ml (¼ pint) dry white wine, see recipe note above
150ml (¼ pint) chicken stock
60ml (4 tbsp) finely chopped fresh parsley

Halve the cucumber and scoop out the seeds. Slice thickly. Trim the escalopes and bat out between sheets of non-stick paper, then season. Heat the butter and oil in a large frying pan and brown the escalopes two at a time. Keep on one side. Add the onion and fry until golden. Stir in the garlic, wine, stock and seasoning. Replace the veal with any juices. Simmer gently uncovered for 10 minutes. Arrange the escalopes in a large serving dish, keep warm. Boil the liquid in the frying pan rapidly to reduce to 60ml (4 tbsp). Add the cucumber and cook, stirring, gently for 5 minutes. Adjust the seasoning and cook for 2 minutes. Stir in the parsley and spoon on either side of the escalopes. Keep warm, covered.

PUREE OF POTATO

King Edward potatoes are best for this recipe because they are a good, floury variety.

1.1kg (2½lb) potatoes, peeled
salt and pepper
50-75g (2-3oz) butter, cut into pieces
300ml (½ pint) hot milk

Cut any large potatoes into even-sized pieces. Cook in salted water for about 15 minutes until tender – test with point of a knife. Drain off all the water, return the pan to a gentle heat for the potatoes to dry. Add the butter and use a potato masher or a fork to mash well. Season to taste. Spread the potatoes in a layer over the pan base. Pour over the hot milk, cover with the lid and leave in a moderately hot place for up to 30 minutes. The potato will take up the liquid. To serve, beat the potatoes well with an electric mixer or balloon whisk until fluffy. Adjust the seasoning.

BUTTERED MANGE-TOUT

Also known as sugar peas, the whole pod is eaten.

700g (1½ lb) mange-tout
25g (1oz) butter

Wash, top and tail the mange-tout. Add to 1cm (½ inch) boiling salted water. Bring back to the boil, cover and simmer for 5 minutes, until just tender. Drain well and toss in the butter, adding plenty of freshly ground black pepper.

FROZEN MERINGUE CREAM

Use homemade meringues as bought ones will over-soften if used in this way.

300ml (½ pint) double cream
125g (4oz) homemade meringues
45ml (3 tbsp) Cointreau

Whip the cream until it holds its shape. Roughly break up the meringues and fold through the cream with the Cointreau. Spoon into a 900ml (1½ pint) soufflé dish. Cover and freeze for at least 6 hours. Serve from the freezer with the spiced plums. Or serve in a 600ml (1 pint) dish prepared in the usual way as for a soufflé.

SPICED RED PLUMS

Firm bottled plums in syrup can be used, but omit the sugar. Use the syrup instead of water and cool before adding the plums.

75g (3oz) soft brown sugar
150ml (¼ pint) port or red wine
5ml (1 level tsp) ground mixed spice
1.25ml (¼ level tsp) ground nutmeg
6 cloves
5cm (2 inch) piece stick cinnamon
300ml (½ pint) water
900g (2lb) ripe red plums, halved and stoned

Place the sugar, port, spices and water into a large shallow saucepan and heat gently until the sugar dissolves. Bring to the boil and simmer for 1 minute. Add the plums to the syrup and bring slowly to the boil. Cover the pan and simmer gently until the plums are just tender. This may take as little as 2-3 minutes, depending on the ripeness of the fruit. Don't overcook as the fruit will continue softening in the heat of the syrup. Pour into a serving dish and cool. Cover with cling film and refrigerate for at least 24 hours. Serve chilled, or reheat gently and serve warm.

COUNTDOWN

The day before: Prepare and freeze the meringue cream. Cook spiced plums; cool, cover and refrigerate.

The morning: Hard-boil the eggs, shell and halve. Prepare the Stilton filling, leave covered in a cool place – don't fill the whites yet. Leave the whites in a bowl of cold water. Sprig the celery leaves, wash, drain and pat dry with absorbent kitchen paper. Store in a polythene bag in the refrigerator. Gently bat out the escalopes between sheets of non-stick paper. Keep in fridge, loosely covered. Peel the potatoes; cut into even-sized pieces and keep covered with cold water. Wash mange-tout. Store in a polythene bag in fridge.

Prepare vegetables for veal dish. Keep covered. Reduce wine if wished.

Chop parsley, keep covered.

To serve at 8pm:

About 6.30pm: Drain and dry the egg whites; pipe the cheese filling into the centre of each, garnish with walnut pieces and refrigerate covered with cling film.

6.30pm: Cover potatoes with fresh, salted water, cover and bring to the boil, reduce heat and simmer gently until tender.

7pm: Drain and purée the potatoes, pour over the hot milk. Cover, leave in a warm place for 30 minutes and beat well.

7.15pm: Preheat the oven. Brown veal and onions, stir in garlic etc., simmer for 10 minutes. Put white wine in refrigerator to chill. Uncork red wine. Take eggs out of refrigerator to come to. Garnish with celery leaves.

7.40pm: Arrange veal on serving plate. Keep warm on side of cooker or in a warm oven. Cook cucumber garnish. Arrange on serving dish with veal and keep warm.

7.50pm: Cook mange-tout. Cover and keep warm. Take desserts from refrigerator.

8pm: Sprinkle potatoes with chopped parsley before serving. Remember to reheat plums if serving warm.

To accompany the veal, we suggest a Beaujolais, in this case a young Fleurie, or a Côte du Rhône, or even an Australian Shiraz.

Watercress & Nutmeg Tart, Monkfish with Prawn Velouté, Len

…achio Rice, Orange & Grape Compote with Brandy Snaps

WINTER DINNER PARTY

MENU FOR SIX

WATERCRESS & NUTMEG TART

The filling of this tart should be only lightly set to get the full flavour of the watercress and nutmeg.

Pastry	125g (4oz) plain white flour
	25g (1oz) plain wholemeal flour · salt and pepper
	75g (3oz) block margarine · 3 eggs, lightly beaten
Filling	bunch watercress, washed, trimmed and finely chopped
	50g (2oz) onion, finely chopped
	30ml (2 level tbsp) chopped fresh parsley
	25g (1oz) butter · 300ml (½ pint) milk
	1.25ml (¼ level tsp) ground nutmeg
Pepper vinaigrette	
	one small red pepper, halved and deseeded
	one small green pepper, halved and deseeded
	45ml (3 tbsp) vinaigrette dressing
	watercress to garnish

For the pastry mix together the white and wholemeal flour with 1.25ml (¼ level tsp) salt. Rub in the margarine until the mixture resembles breadcrumbs. Pour about 30ml (2 tbsp) egg into the dry ingredients, enough to form a firm dough. On a lightly floured surface, quickly knead the pastry to a smooth ball. Wrap and chill for 10-15 minutes. Place a 20.5cm (8 inch) flan ring on a baking tray. Roll out the pastry thinly and use to line the flan ring. Cover the base with foil and fill with baking beans. Bake 'blind' in the oven, 200°C conventional oven/180°C fan oven/1st shelf, for about 15 minutes, until the pastry is well dried out but not browned. Remove the foil and beans during the final 5 minutes cooking time. Melt the butter in a small frying pan and sauté the watercress, onion and parsley for 4-5 minutes, until the onion is golden. Whisk together the milk, remaining egg and ground nutmeg. Stir in the sautéed mixture. Season and pour into the prepared pastry case. Bake in the oven, 180°C conventional oven/160°C fan oven/1st shelf, for about 20-35 minutes, until just set. Cut the red and green peppers into thin, matchstick-sized pieces. Toss in the vinaigrette dressing. Serve the tart warm garnished with watercress, accompanied by the pepper vinaigrette.

MONKFISH WITH PRAWN VELOUTE

Monkfish is a deep sea fish and only the tail is used. Its flesh is firm, white and succulent, and said to resemble lobster or scampi.

6 skinned monkfish fillets, about 200g (7oz) each
75g (3oz) butter
50g (2oz) mushrooms, wiped and finely chopped
50g (2oz) shallot or onion, finely chopped
45ml (3 tbsp) white wine vinegar
300ml (½ pint) dry white wine
2 bay leaves · 150ml (¼ pint) water
125g (4oz) cooked prawns with shells
25g (1oz) plain flour · 5ml (1 level tsp) tomato purée
5ml (1 tsp) lemon juice · salt and pepper
6 cooked prawns with shells, to garnish

Trim the monkfish of any loose skin. Place the fillets in a shallow ovenproof dish large enough to hold the fillets in one layer. Melt 25g (1oz) of the butter in a saucepan and sauté the mushrooms and shallot or onion for 2-3 minutes until golden. Add the white wine vinegar, white wine, bay leaves and water. Bring to the boil, simmer uncovered for 2 minutes. Strain over the monkfish fillets. Cover tightly. Bake in the oven, 180°C conventional oven/160°C fan oven/3rd shelf, for about 30-40 minutes, until just cooked. Wash and shell the prawns. Refrigerate the flesh and reserve the shells. Melt 25g (1oz) of the remaining butter in a saucepan and stir in the prawn shells. Cook, stirring, for 1-2 minutes, then add the flour and tomato purée. Cook for a further 1-2 minutes. Remove from the heat. Strain the cooking liquid from the monkfish. Cover the fish tightly and return to a very slow oven, 130°C conventional oven/110°C fan oven/1st shelf, to keep warm. Return the prawn mixture to the heat, whisk in 450ml (¾ pint) strained cooking liquid and the lemon juice. Bring to the boil and simmer for 1-2 minutes. Pureé in a blender until smooth; strain back into the saucepan, whisk in the remaining butter and season. Spoon over the monkfish fillets. Cover and keep warm in the slow oven. To serve, garnish with the shelled and unshelled prawns.

LEMON PISTACHIO RICE

If possible, use Italian long-grain rice.

25g (1oz) shelled pistachio nuts
350g (12oz) long-grain rice
grated rind and juice of 1 lemon · butter
750ml (1¼ pint) water · salt and pepper

Dip the pistachio nuts into boiling water for 5-10 seconds. Drain; rub off the outer skins. With a small sharp knife, cut each nut into long slivers. Place the rice, nuts and lemon rind into a well-buttered 2 litre (3½ pint) shallow ovenproof dish. Bring the water, lemon juice, 10ml (2 level tsp) salt and some pepper to the boil, pour over the rice. Stir well. Cover tightly with a lid or foil. Bake in the oven 180°C conventional oven/160°C fan oven/1st shelf for about 30-40 minutes, until the grains are just soft and the cooking liquid has all been absorbed by the rice. Keep warm in a very slow oven until ready to serve. Alternatively, cook ahead and cool. Cover with well-buttered foil. Reheat in the oven, 180°C conventional oven/160°C fan oven/1st shelf, for about 35-40 minutes. Stir before serving.

STEAMED LEEKS

A saucepan with a tightly fitting lid ensures that the vegetables are steamed rather than boiled.

1.4kg (3lb) leeks, trimmed · salt and pepper
ground nutmeg · 75ml (3fl oz) light stock

Thinly slice the leeks, then wash well. Place the leeks in a large saucepan with a tightly fitting lid. Season with salt, pepper and nutmeg. Pour in the stock. Cover and cook over a medium heat for 5-7 minutes, until the leeks are tender.

ORANGE & GRAPE COMPOTE

Choose fleshy, juicy oranges for this compote. Make sure they are the thin-skinned type and not the sort with a thick layer of pith.

50-75g (2-3oz) granulated sugar · 300ml (½ pint) water
30ml (2 tbsp) strained lemon juice
6 large seedless oranges
225g (8oz) black grapes, halved and pipped

Place the sugar and water in a small saucepan and warm gently until the sugar dissolves. Bring to the boil and simmer for 2 minutes. Cool, then stir in the lemon juice. Pare off a few strips of orange rind using a potato peeler, scrape off any white pith and slice the rind into fine shreds. Place in a small pan of boiling water and boil for 1 minute, strain and cool. Using a serrated knife, cut away all the rind and pith from the oranges – prepare these over the glass serving bowl to catch any juices. Slice the oranges into narrow rounds. Mix the grapes and oranges together in the serving bowl. Pour over the cool syrup, cover and chill well before serving. Decorate with the shredded orange rind.

BRANDY SNAPS

If you don't possess enough wooden spoons, a finger-thick piece of dowel can be used.

50g (2oz) golden syrup · 50g (2oz) caster sugar
50g (2oz) butter or block margarine
50g (2oz) plain flour
2.5ml (½ level tsp) ground ginger
finely grated rind of ½ lemon · 30ml (2 tbsp) brandy
300ml (½ pint) double cream
15ml (1 level tbsp) sifted icing sugar

Place the syrup, sugar and butter in a small heavy-based saucepan and warm gently until the sugar dissolves and the butter melts. Remove the pan from the heat. Sift the flour and ground ginger together and stir into the pan with the lemon rind and 5ml (1 tsp) of the brandy. Using about 10ml (2 level tsp) of the mixture for each snap, spoon out on to two baking trays lined with non-stick paper. Since the brandy snaps spread, allow not more than six to a tray. Bake in the oven, 180°C conventional oven/160°C fan oven/1st and 2nd shelf, for about 7-10 minutes, until surfaces are bubbly and golden brown. Leave the snaps to firm up slightly about 1 minute – then roll loosely around the greased handles of wooden spoons. Leave to set on a wire rack then ease out the spoons. Stiffly whip the cream and whisk in the remaining brandy and the icing sugar. Spoon the cream into a piping bag fitted with a 5mm (¼ inch) star vegetable nozzle. Pipe the cream into either end of the snaps and pile up on a serving dish. Stand this in a cool place for 2 hours before serving. Alternatively, the cream may be served separately.

COUNTDOWN

The day before: Make the brandy snaps, cool, do not fill yet. Store in an airtight container. They can be made up to a week ahead. Make the pastry for the Watercress and Nutmeg Tart. Line the flan ring and bake 'blind'. Cool on the baking tray. Leave, loosely covered, in a cool place. Prepare the filling; sauté the onion, watercress and parsley, then stir into the milk, egg and nutmeg mixture. Cover and refrigerate. Deseed the peppers; cut into thin match-stick pieces; toss in the vinaigrette dressing. Cover and refrigerate. Prepare the cooking liquid for the monkfish. Sauté the chopped mushrooms and shallot or onion. Add the white wine vinegar, wine, bay leaves and water. Cool, cover, and refrigerate. Shell the prawns. Place shells and flesh in separate polythene bags; refrigerate. Skin the pistachio nuts; keep in a polythene bag.
The morning: Cook the tart. When quite cold cover loosely with foil. Keep in a cool place, on its baking sheet. Slice the leeks; wash and drain. Keep refrigerated in a polythene bag. Cook the rice. Cool, re-cover with well-buttered foil and refrigerate. Prepare the orange and grape compote, cover and chill. Blanch the needle shreds of orange rind, drain, pat dry and keep in a polythene bag.
To serve at 8pm: About 5pm: Fill the brandy snaps with cream and leave in a cool place.
6.45pm: Preheat the oven. Place leeks and stock in saucepan. and cover. Remove pepper vinaigrette from refrigerator.
7pm: Bring cooking liquid for fish to the boil. Strain over the monkfish fillets. Cover tightly. Bake in the oven for about 35-40 minutes. Place rice in oven to reheat. Chill wine.
7.35pm: Begin the fish sauce; sauté prawn shells in the butter, add flour and tomato purée, remove from heat. Strain the juices from fish. Re-cover fish, return to a very slow oven. Place loosely covered watercress tart in oven to warm. Put prawn mixture back over heat. Finish the fish sauce. Spoon over monkfish. Re-cover and keep warm. Stir rice; replace foil and keep warm. Put leeks on to cook. Garnish and serve watercress tart and pepper vinaigrette. Decorate the compote with orange rind for serving.
To accompany the fish, why not try a well-chilled German white, such as the 1976 Ruppertsberger Riesling, or more conventionally, a dry or medium white from France.

Casseroles

Chilli con Carne

CHILLI CON CARNE
Serves 4-6

| 125g (4oz) dried kidney beans |
| 15g (½oz) lard |
| 700g (1½lb) good quality lean minced beef |
| 225g (8oz) onions, chopped |
| 5ml (1 level tsp) ground ginger |
| 2.5ml (½ level tsp) ground cumin |
| 4ml (¾ level tsp) chilli powder |
| 15ml (1 level tbsp) plain flour |
| 40ml (2½ level tbsp) treacle |
| 150ml (¼ pint) stock |
| 30ml (2 tbsp) red wine |
| one 152g (5oz) can tomato purée |
| one 300g (11oz) can tomatoes |
| salt and pepper |
| half 190g (6¾oz) can pimento, drained and finely chopped |
| chopped fresh parsley, to garnish |

Cover the beans with cold water, soak overnight, drain. Put into a pan with fresh water and simmer for 20-30 minutes until beginning to soften, drain. In a large frying pan, melt the lard and brown the mince well. Remove to a casserole using a slotted draining spoon. In the same pan, brown the onions. Add the ginger, cumin, chilli powder and flour. Cook, stirring, for 2 minutes. Add mince and all the other ingredients except the pimento. Bring to the boil, then put into casserole. Cover and cook in oven for about 1¾ hours, until the beans are tender. Just before serving, skim and stir in the pimento. Garnish with parsley. Instead of dried kidney beans, use one 432g (15¼oz) can, drain the beans and add to the minced beef with the pimento. Continue cooking about 10 minutes until hot.

Oven	Conventional	Fan
Temperature	170°C	150°C
Preheating	Recommended	Not necessary
Shelf position	1st	1st
Time	2 hours	1¾ hours

OLDE ENGLISH PORK CASSEROLE
Serves 4

| 25g (1oz) lard |
| 175g (6oz) leeks, trimmed, washed and chopped |
| 550g (1¼lb) shoulder of pork, cut into 2.5cm (1 inch) pieces |
| 25g (1oz) seasoned flour |
| 300ml (½ pint) cider |
| dash of Tabasco sauce |
| piece of lemon rind |
| 75g (3oz) button mushrooms |
| bouquet garni |
| salt and pepper |

Melt the lard in a flameproof casserole and fry the leeks for a few minutes. Meanwhile, toss the pork in the seasoned flour. Add to the leeks and cook for 5 minutes. Add the cider, Tabasco sauce, lemon rind, mushrooms and bouquet garni. Bring to the boil. Cover and cook in the oven for about 1 hour, until the pork is tender. Remove the bouquet garni. Season to taste. Serve with mashed potatoes and buttered carrots.

Oven	Conventional	Fan
Temperature	180°C	160°C
Preheating	Recommended	Not necessary
Shelf position	1st	1st
Time	1¼ hours	1 hour

HUNGARIAN GOULASH
Serves 4

| 15ml (1 tbsp) olive oil |
| 700g (1½lb) chuck steak, trimmed and cut into 4cm (1½ inch) cubes |
| 2 large onions, roughly chopped |
| one garlic clove, skinned and crushed |
| 30ml (2 level tbsp) plain flour |
| 30ml (2 level tbsp) Hungarian paprika |
| one 400g (14oz) can tomatoes |
| salt and pepper |
| one medium green or red pepper, halved, seeded and cut into 5cm (2 inch) strips |
| one 142ml (5 fl oz) carton soured cream |
| extra paprika, to sprinkle |

Heat the oil in a flameproof casserole until sizzling hot and brown the cubes of beef on all sides, cooking a few at a time and transferring them to a plate as they brown. Reduce the heat to medium, stir in the onions and cook for about 5 minutes or until a pale golden colour. Add the garlic and return the meat to the casserole. Sprinkle in the flour and paprika and stir to soak up the juices. Add the tomatoes, seasoning and bring slowly to simmering point. Cover with a tight-fitting lid and cook in the oven for about 2 hours. Stir in the pepper strips, replace the lid and cook for a further 30 minutes or until the meat is tender. Just before serving, stir in the soured cream to give a marbled, creamy effect, then sprinkle a little more paprika over. Serve straight from the casserole, with cooked rice and vegetables.

Oven	Conventional	Fan
Temperature	160°C	140°C
Preheating	Recommended	Not necessary
Shelf position	1st	1st
Time	2½ hours	2¼ hours

CALCUTTA SPICED BEEF
Serves 3-4

5ml (1 level tsp) ground coriander
5ml (1 level tsp) ground turmeric
5ml (1 level tsp) ground chilli
pinch of black pepper
pinch of ground ginger
125ml (¼ pint) coconut milk, see below
25g (1oz) butter
one onion, sliced
one garlic clove, skinned and crushed
450g (1lb) stewing steak, trimmed and cubed
200ml (⅓ pint) stock
salt
lemon juice

Mix together the spices and make into a paste with a little of the coconut milk. Melt the butter in a flameproof casserole and fry the onion and garlic until tender. Add the paste and fry for a further 3-4 minutes. Add the meat and stock, bring slowly to the boil. Cover and cook in the oven for about 2¼ hours, until the beef is tender. Add the remaining coconut milk, some salt and lemon juice to taste. Serve at once, accompanied by boiled rice and a fruit or vegetable sambal.
Coconut Milk: Traditionally made from fresh coconut but a good substitute can be gained by infusing 15ml (1 level tbsp) desiccated coconut in about 125ml (¼ pint) boiling water, then squeezing out the liquid through a fine tea strainer.

Oven	Conventional	Fan
Temperature	170°C	150°C
Preheating	Recommended	Not necessary
Shelf position	1st	1st
Time	2½ hours	2¼ hours

BEEF BOURGUIGNONNE
Serves 4

25g (1oz) beef dripping or lard
900g (2lb) chuck steak, trimmed and cubed
125g (4oz) streaky bacon, chopped
30ml (2 level tbsp) plain flour
salt and pepper
450ml (¾ pint) red wine
bouquet garni
15g (½oz) butter
225g (8oz) small pickling onions
225g (8oz) button mushrooms
5ml (1 level tsp) soft dark brown sugar
5ml (1 level tsp) mustard

Melt the fat in a large flameproof casserole and quickly brown the meat. Remove with a slotted draining spoon. Add the bacon and fry for 2-3 minutes until crisp. Remove from the pan. Stir the flour into the remaining fat and cook for a few minutes, then gradually blend in 300ml (½ pint) of the wine. Return the meat and bacon to the pan and add the bouquet garni. Cover and cook in the oven for about 2 hours. Melt the butter in a small pan and fry the onions and mushrooms gently for 2-3 minutes. Pour in the remaining wine, sugar and mustard and bring to the boil. Stir into the casserole and continue to cook in the oven for the remaining time, or until the meat and onions are tender. Discard the bouquet garni and adjust the seasoning before serving.

Oven	Conventional	Fan
Temperature	160°C	140°C
Preheating	Recommended	Not necessary
Shelf position	1st	1st
Time	2½ hours	2¼ hours

Top: Lancashire Hotpot   Bottom: Duckling with Peach Sauce

CASSEROLES

LANCASHIRE HOTPOT
Serves 4-6

one kg (2lb) potatoes, peeled and sliced
salt and pepper
beef dripping or lard, to fry
one kg (2lb) middle neck lamb chops
2 lamb's kidneys, cleaned and chopped
one large onion, sliced
2.5ml (½ level tsp) dried thyme
600ml (1 pint) hot beef stock

Put half the potato slices in a layer on the base of a deep casserole. Season well with salt and pepper. Melt a knob of dripping or lard in a frying pan and quickly brown the chops and kidneys on all sides. Remove from the pan with a slotted draining spoon. Lay the chops and kidneys on top of the potatoes, add the onion and sprinkle with the thyme. Pour in the hot stock. Put the remaining potatoes in a layer on top. Season again. Cover and bake in the oven for about 2 hours. Remove the lid and return to the oven to brown the top layer of potatoes for 15-20 minutes. Serve immediately, straight from the casserole, with a seasonal green vegetable or buttered carrots.

Oven	Conventional	Fan
Temperature	180°C	160°C
Preheating	Recommended	Not necessary
Shelf position	1st	1st
Time	2½ hours	2¼ hours

DUCKLING WITH PEACH SAUCE
Serves 4

4 duckling joints, about 350g (12oz) each
15ml (1 tbsp) vegetable oil
25g (1oz) butter
salt and pepper
300ml (½ pint) dry white wine
rosemary sprig or 1.25ml (¼ level tsp) dried
3 fresh firm peaches, halved and stoned
15ml (1 tbsp) brandy
10ml (2 level tsp) arrowroot
15ml (1 tbsp) water
fresh rosemary sprigs or watercress, to garnish

Trim any excess fat from the duckling joints. Heat the oil and butter in a large, shallow flameproof casserole and fry the joints for 10 minutes to brown all over. Remove from the pan. Pour off the fat and wipe the casserole. Return the joints to the pan, season well. Pour over the wine and add the rosemary. Arrange the peaches on the duckling. Cover tightly and bake in the oven for about 30 minutes. Remove the skin from four peach halves, reserve two halves, unpeeled, for garnish. Replace the skinned peaches in the casserole and continue cooking until the duckling is tender. Lift the duckling from the pan juices, keep warm. Discard the rosemary sprig. Lay several sheets of absorbent kitchen paper over juices to absorb as much fat as possible. Pour the brandy into a pan, gently warm and flambé, then pour into the juices. Blend the arrowroot and water together, stir into bubbling juices. Bring to the boil and replace the duckling. Peel and slice the remaining peach halves, add to the casserole. Garnish with fresh rosemary sprigs or watercress.

Oven	Conventional	Fan
Temperature	170°C	150°C
Preheating	Recommended	Not necessary
Shelf position	1st	1st
Time	1½ hours	1¼ hours

ITALIAN VEAL CASSEROLE
Serves 4

700g (1½lb) boned leg of veal
60ml (2 tbsp) vegetable oil
2 garlic cloves, skinned and chopped
salt and pepper
225g (8oz) tomatoes, skinned and chopped
10ml (2 level tsp) tomato purée
150ml (¼ pint) white wine
2 sprigs of rosemary
strip of lemon rind

Slice the meat or cut into small pieces. Heat the oil in a frying pan and fry the garlic for about 2 minutes until golden brown. Add the meat, salt and pepper and cook for about 8-10 minutes until the meat is golden brown. Stir in the tomatoes, tomato purée, wine, rosemary and lemon rind. Add just enough water to cover. Pour into a casserole, cover tightly and cook in the oven for about 1 hour, or until the meat is tender.

Oven	Conventional	Fan
Temperature	180°C	150°C
Preheating	Recommended	Not necessary
Shelf position	1st	1st
Time	1 hour	1 hour

CASSEROLES

CHICKEN MARENGO

Serves 4

30ml (2 tbsp) vegetable oil
4 chicken joints
2 carrots, peeled and sliced
one stick of celery, trimmed and chopped
one onion, chopped
50g (2oz) streaky bacon, rinded and chopped
45ml (3 level tbsp) plain flour
300ml (½ pint) chicken stock
one 425g (15oz) can tomatoes
30ml (2 tbsp) sherry
salt and pepper
bouquet garni
125g (4oz) mushrooms, sliced
12 black olives, stoned
chopped fresh parsley, to garnish

Heat the oil in a frying pan and fry the chicken joints for about 5 minutes until golden brown. Remove from the pan and put into a casserole. Fry the vegetables and bacon in the oil for about 5 minutes until golden brown. Remove from the pan. Stir the flour into the remaining fat, cook for 2-3 minutes and gradually stir in the stock. Bring to the boil and continue to stir until thickened. Return the vegetables to the pan and add the tomatoes, sherry, salt and pepper. Pour this sauce over the chicken joints, add the bouquet garni and mushrooms. Cook in the oven for about 50 minutes, until the chicken joints are tender. Stir in the olives. Remove the joints to a warmed serving dish. Strain the sauce from the casserole over them and sprinkle with chopped parsley.

Oven	Conventional	Fan
Temperature	180°C	160°C
Preheating	Recommended	Not necessary
Shelf position	1st	1st
Time	1 hour	50 minutes

CASSEROLED SPAGHETTI CHEESE WITH HADDOCK

Serves 4-6

175g (6oz) wholewheat spaghetti rings
175g (6oz) spring onions or shallots, roughly chopped
75g (3oz) butter or margarine
60ml (4 level tbsp) plain flour
900ml (1½ pints) milk
salt and pepper
225g (8oz) grated Edam cheese
175g (6oz) smoked haddock fillet, skinned
25g (1oz) fresh white breadcrumbs

Cook the spaghetti rings in a saucepan of boiling salted water for 10 minutes. Drain well. Melt the butter in a large saucepan and sauté the onions until softened. Stir in the flour, milk and seasoning and bring to the boil. Simmer for 1 minute, stirring. Remove from the heat and stir in three-quarters of the grated cheese, then add the spaghetti rings and flaked haddock. Turn into a shallow casserole. Combine the remaining grated cheese with the crumbs and sprinkle over the spaghetti rings mixture. Bake in the oven for about 30 minutes.

Oven	Conventional	Fan
Temperature	200°C	180°C
Preheating	Recommended	Not necessary
Shelf position	1st	1st
Time	35 minutes	30 minutes

VEAL WITH PAPRIKA

Serves 4-6

4 streaky bacon rashers, rinded and diced
2 medium onions, sliced
30ml (2 tbsp) vegetable oil
700g (1½lb) shoulder of veal, boned and cubed
300ml (½ pint) chicken stock
20ml (4 level tsp) paprika
25g (1oz) butter
175g (6oz) button mushrooms
one 142ml (5floz) carton soured cream
30ml (2 tbsp) flaked almonds, lightly toasted

Place the bacon in a frying pan and fry in its own fat until crisp. Remove from the pan. Fry the onions in the bacon fat for about 5 minutes until soft and golden brown. Discard the bacon fat. Heat the oil in the pan, then

CASSEROLES

brown the veal a few cubes at a time. Put the bacon, onion and veal in a 2 litre (3½ pint) casserole. Pour on the stock, mixed with the paprika. Cover and cook in the oven for about 45 minutes. Meanwhile, heat the butter in a pan and fry the mushrooms. Add to the veal with the soured cream. Return the casserole to the oven and cook for a further 30 minutes. Adjust the seasoning, sprinkle the almonds on top and serve accompanied by plain noodles or boiled potatoes.

Oven	Conventional	Fan
Temperature	170°C	150°C
Preheating	Recommended	Not necessary
Shelf position	1st	1st
Time	1¼ hours	1 hour

CIDER-BAKED RABBIT WITH CABBAGE

Serves 8

225g (8oz) streaky bacon rashers, rinded
60ml (4 tbsp) vegetable oil
225g (8oz) onion, sliced
350g (12oz) cooking apples, peeled and sliced
900g (2lb) firm white cabbage, coarsely shredded
salt and pepper
8 rabbit joints, about 1.4kg (3lb) total weight
60ml (4 level tbsp) plain flour
15ml (3 level tsp) French mustard
300ml (½ pint) dry cider
450ml (¾ pint) light stock
chopped fresh parsley, to garnish

Snip the bacon into small pieces. Heat the oil in a large frying pan and lightly brown the bacon, onion and apple. Lift out of the pan with a slotted draining spoon, mix with the cabbage and plenty of seasoning. Place in a large ovenproof casserole. Reheat the remaining oil and brown the rabbit joints well. Place on top of the cabbage. Stir the flour and mustard into the pan. Gradually add the cider and stock, stirring. Season and bring to the boil. Pour over the rabbit; cover tightly and cook in the oven for about 1¼ hours, or until the rabbit is tender. Adjust the seasoning. Garnish with plenty of parsley.

Oven	Conventional	Fan
Temperature	170°C	150°C
Preheating	Recommended	Not necessary
Shelf position	1st	1st
Time	1½ hours	1¼ hours

BACON STEW WITH DUMPLINGS

Serves 6

900g (2lb) smoked bacon fore-end joint
45ml (3 tbsp) vegetable oil
45ml (3 level tbsp) plain flour
600ml (1 pint) unseasoned stock
5ml (1 level tsp) dried mixed herbs
450g (1lb) leeks, trimmed and sliced into 1cm (½ inch) pieces
pepper

Dumplings

125g (4oz) self raising flour
50g (2oz) shredded suet
45ml (3 tbsp) chopped fresh parsley

Cut the bacon into 5cm (2 inch) pieces, discarding the skin. Put into a pan of cold water, bring to the boil and blanch for 1 minute. Drain and rinse under cold running water. Heat the oil in a flameproof casserole and brown the bacon. Stir in the plain flour, stock, mixed herbs and bring to the boil. Add the leeks and season. Cover and cook in the oven for about 1 hour. For the dumplings, mix together the self raising flour, suet and parsley. Bind with water to a firm but manageable dough and shape into six dumplings. Add the dumplings to the casserole, replace the lid and continue to cook for a further 20 minutes at 200°C Conventional/175°C Fan, or until the bacon is tender and the dumplings 'puffed up'.

Oven	Conventional	Fan
Temperature	170°C	150°C
Preheating	Recommended	Not necessary
Shelf position	1st	1st
Time	1½ hours	1¼ hours

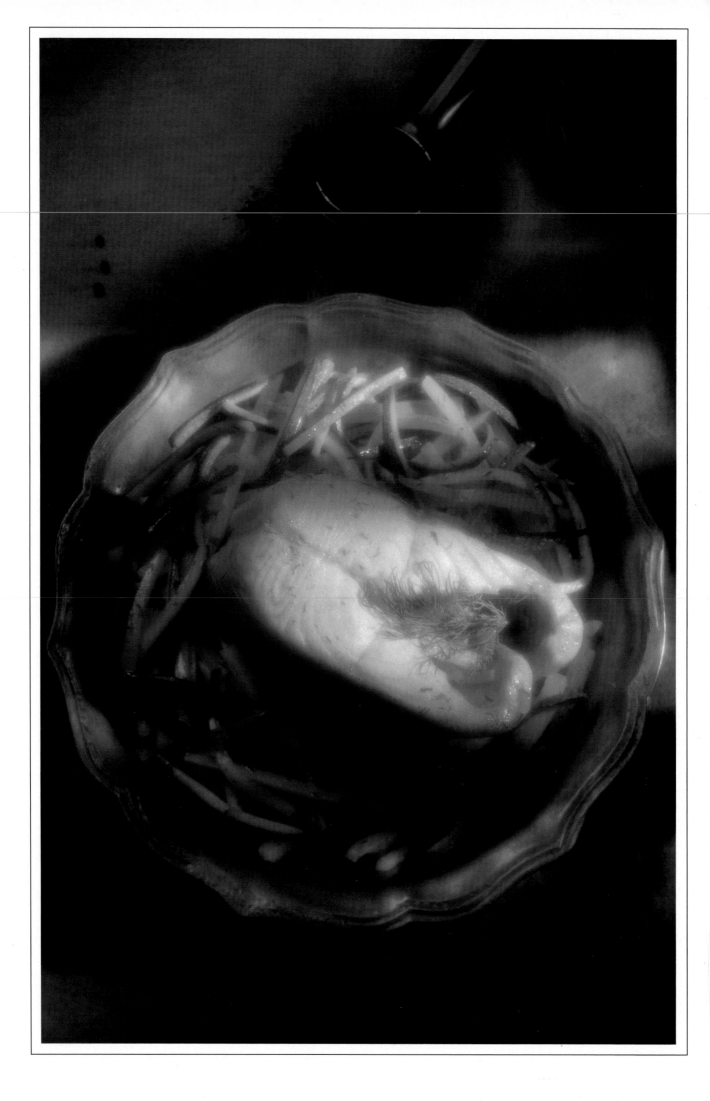

BAKED SALMON AND DILL

Serves 4

700g (1½lb) piece middle cut salmon
50g (2oz) butter
175g (6oz) carrots, peeled and cut into thin strips
175g (6oz) celery, washed, trimmed and cut into thin strips
225g (8oz) courgettes, trimmed and cut into thin strips
2.5ml (½ level tsp) dried dill weed
salt and pepper
45ml (3 tbsp) lemon juice
fresh dill, to garnish

Rinse the salmon and pat dry with absorbent kitchen paper. Melt the butter in a medium flameproof casserole and stir the vegetables over a high heat for 2-3 minutes. Mix in the dill. Place the fish on top of the vegetables, season well and pour over the lemon juice. Press a piece of damp greaseproof paper on top of the fish. Cover with a close-fitting lid. Bake in the oven for about 30 minutes, until the vegetables are tender and the fish flakes easily. Lift the fish on to a warmed serving dish and ease off the skin. Surround with the vegetables and spoon over the juices. Garnish with fresh dill.

Oven	Conventional	Fan
Temperature	170°C	150°C
Preheating	Recommended	Not necessary
Shelf position	1st	1st
Time	40 minutes	30 minutes

COURGETTE AND TOMATO AU GRATIN

Serves 4

40g (1½oz) butter
60ml (4 level tbsp) plain flour
400ml (¾ pint) milk
150g (5oz) grated Cheddar cheese
5ml (1 level tsp) dry mustard
salt and pepper
450g (1lb) leeks, trimmed, washed and thinly sliced
450g (1lb) courgettes, trimmed and cut into 5mm (¼ inch) slices
450g (1lb) tomatoes, skinned and sliced
25g (1oz) fresh white breadcrumbs

Melt the butter in a saucepan, stir in the flour and cook for 1 minute. Remove the pan from the heat and gradually stir in the milk. Bring to the boil, stirring, and cook for 1 minute until thickened. Stir in 125g (4oz) of the cheese, the mustard and seasoning. Arrange the leeks, courgettes, tomatoes and the cheese sauce in layers in a greased 1.4 litre (2½ pint) ovenproof dish, seasoning the courgettes and tomatoes. Finish with a layer of cheese sauce. Stir the remaining cheese and the breadcrumbs together and spoon over the top. Cook in the oven for about 50 minutes, until the vegetables are tender and the top golden brown.

Oven	Conventional	Fan
Temperature	190°C	170°C
Preheating	Not necessary	Not necessary
Shelf position	2nd	1st
Time	1 hour	50 minutes

MIXED BEAN CASSEROLE

Serves 4-6

125g (4oz) dried haricot beans
125g (4oz) dried black-eyed beans
125g (4oz) dried red lentils
30-45ml (2-3 tbsp) vegetable oil
450g (1lb) onions, sliced
4 sticks of celery, trimmed and sliced
2 garlic cloves, skinned and crushed
5ml (1 level tsp) dried thyme
5ml (1 level tsp) dried oregano
30ml (2 level tbsp) chopped fresh parsley
900ml (1½ pints) beef stock
5-7.5ml (1-1½ level tsp) yeast extract
salt and pepper
chopped fresh parsley, to garnish

Soak the beans and lentils in cold water overnight. Drain. Heat the oil in a flameproof casserole and cook the onions until softened and lightly browned. Stir in the celery, drained beans and lentils, garlic, thyme, oregano, parsley, stock, yeast extract and seasoning. Bring to the boil, cover and cook in the oven for about 1¾ hours, until all the beans are tender. Serve sprinkled with parsley.

Oven	Conventional	Fan
Temperature	170°C	150°C
Preheating	Recommended	Not necessary
Shelf position	1st	1st
Time	2 hours	1¾ hours

Left: Baked Salmon and Dill

CASSEROLES

RED CABBAGE CASSEROLE

Serves 4

| 2 cooking apples, peeled, cored and sliced |
| 700g (1½lb) red cabbage, trimmed and thinly sliced |
| one large onion, thinly sliced |
| 50g (2oz) raisins |
| 10ml (2 level tsp) sugar |
| salt and pepper |
| 300ml (½ pint) dry white wine or chicken stock |
| 25g (1oz) butter |

Put the apples in a casserole with the red cabbage, onion, raisins, sugar and salt and pepper to taste. Pour in the wine or stock, or a mixture of both, and stir well to mix. Cover the casserole with a lid or buttered greaseproof paper or foil and bake in the oven for about 1 hour, or until the cabbage is tender. Adjust the seasoning and stir in the butter until melted. Serve straight from the casserole.

Oven	Conventional	Fan
Temperature	170°C	150°C
Preheating	Recommended	Not necessary
Shelf position	1st	1st
Time	1¼ hours	1 hour

RATATOUILLE

Serves 4-6

| 30ml (2 tbsp) vegetable oil |
| 15g (½ oz) butter |
| 2 large onions, sliced |
| one large aubergine, chopped |
| 4 tomatoes, skinned and chopped |
| 4 courgettes, trimmed and sliced |
| one green or red pepper, deseeded and sliced |
| one garlic clove, skinned and crushed |
| 30ml (2 level tbsp) tomato purée |
| salt and pepper |
| 15ml (1 tbsp) chopped parsley |

Heat the oil and butter in a flameproof casserole and add the prepared vegetables, tomato purée and seasoning. Stir well, cover tightly and bake in the oven for about 1 hour, until the vegetables are tender. Serve hot, sprinkled with parsley, and accompanied by French bread.

Oven	Conventional	Fan
Temperature	180°C	160°C
Preheating	Recommended	Not necessary
Shelf position	1st	1st
Time	1¼ hours	1 hour

AUBERGINE AND TOMATO CASSEROLE

Serves 4

| 2 large aubergines, about 700g (1½lb), sliced |
| salt and pepper |
| butter and vegetable or cooking oil, to fry |
| one large onion, thinly sliced |
| one garlic clove, skinned and crushed (optional) |
| one 396g (14oz) can tomatoes, sieved |
| 15ml (1 level tbsp) tomato purée |
| 5ml (1 level tsp) chopped fresh oregano or basil, or 2.5ml (½ level tsp) dried |
| 2.5ml (½ level tsp) sugar |
| 150ml (¼ pint) natural yoghurt |
| 25g (1oz) grated Parmesan cheese |
| 25g (1oz) fresh white breadcrumbs |

Degorge the aubergine slices by sprinkling with salt and leaving to 'sweat' for 30 minutes, then rinse and dry thoroughly. Heat a knob of butter and a spoonful of oil in a large frying pan. When foaming, add enough aubergines slices to cover the bottom of the pan. Fry until browned on both sides, then remove from the pan with a slotted spoon and drain on absorbent kitchen paper. Fry the remaining aubergine slices in this way, adding more oil and butter when necessary. Fry the onion and garlic (if using) in the same pan until golden. Stir in the sieved tomatoes, tomato purée, oregano or basil, sugar and seasoning to taste. Bring to the boil, then lower the heat and simmer for about 5 minutes to reduce the sauce slightly. Divide the aubergines into three equal portions and put one portion in the bottom of a shallow oven-proof dish. Divide the tomato sauce into two and put one half on top of the aubergines. Repeat these three layers once more, cover with yoghurt then finish with the grated Parmesan and breadcrumbs. Bake in the oven for about 45 minutes, or until the topping is golden brown and bubbling.

Oven	Conventional	Fan
Temperature	170°C	150°C
Preheating	Recommended	Not necessary
Shelf position	1st	1st
Time	1 hour	40-45 minutes

Red Cabbage Casserole

Savoury Suppers

PICNIC LOAF

Serves 6-8

Filling

450g (1lb) belly pork, skinned and boned
125g (4oz) lean bacon rashers
salt and pepper
4 eggs, hard boiled

Pastry

125g (4oz) lard
150ml (¼ pint) water
350g (12oz) plain flour
5ml (1 level tsp) salt
one egg, beaten

Jelly

150ml (¼ pint) stock
15ml (1 level tbsp) powdered gelatine

For the filling, mince the pork and bacon. Add seasoning. For the pastry, heat the lard and water in a saucepan until the lard melts and water boils. Sift the flour and salt into a bowl. Add the boiled liquid and mix evenly into the flour. Knead lightly to a smooth dough. Take two-thirds of the dough and press it into a 900g (2lb) loaf tin, lining evenly. Roll out or shape remaining third for the lid. Spread half the pork filling into the pastry case. Arrange the eggs on top, press in the remaining pork mixture. Brush the pastry edges with egg, seal the lid in position. Make holes in the lid and brush with egg. Bake in the oven at the higher temperature for about 20 minutes, then at the lower temperature for about 40 minutes. Leave until cool. Dissolve the gelatine in the stock, pour through a funnel through a hole in the pastry lid. Chill until cold and firm.

Oven	Conventional	Fan
Temperature	200°C reduce to 180°C	180°C reduce to 160°C
Preheating	Recommended	Not necessary
Shelf position	1st	1st
Time	1¼ hours	1 hour

CHICKEN PIE

Serves 6

1.8kg (4lb) oven-ready chicken
one small onion, halved
one carrot, peeled
one leek, washed and trimmed, or 1 stick of celery, washed
6 peppercorns
salt and pepper

Sauce

50g (2oz) butter
175g (6oz) onion, chopped
225g (8oz) sweet red peppers, seeded and finely chopped
50g (2oz) green chillies, halved and seeded
75ml (4 level tbsp) plain flour
600ml (1 pint) chicken stock
125g (4oz) grated mature Cheddar cheese
puff pastry, made with 175g (6oz) flour, or 375g (13oz) frozen puff pastry, thawed
one egg, beaten

Place the chicken in a saucepan with sufficient water to cover and add the onion, carrot, leek or celery, peppercorns and salt. Simmer for about 2 hours. Remove the chicken, reduce the liquor to 600ml (1 pint) by rapid boiling, then strain. For the sauce, melt the butter in a pan and fry the onion, peppers and chillies for 10 minutes; if wished, the chillies may by removed at this stage. Carve the chicken, cutting it into fork-size pieces, and discard the skin. Place the chicken in a 1.7-litre (3 pint) pie dish with a funnel. Blend the flour into the fried vegetables and slowly add the strained stock, stirring continuously. Bring to the boil. When the liquid has thickened, add the cheese and adjust the seasoning. Spoon over the chicken and leave to cool. Roll out the puff pastry and use to cover the pie. Knock up and scallop the edge and score the top of the pastry into diamonds with a knife. Brush with beaten egg and place on the oven baking tray. Cook in the oven at the higher temperature for about 25 minutes, until the pastry is colouring, then at the lower temperature for about 25 minutes, until well risen and browned.

Oven	Conventional	Fan
Temperature	220°C reduce to 170°C	200°C reduce to 150°C
Preheating	Recommended	Recommended
Shelf position	1st	1st
Time	1 hour	50 minutes

Cheese Soufflé

Lasagne al Forno

LASAGNE AL FORNO

Serves 4-6

olive oil, to fry
one large onion, chopped
one garlic clove, skinned and crushed with 2.5ml (½ level tsp) salt
2 sticks of celery, washed and finely chopped
125g (4oz) unsmoked streaky bacon, rinded and chopped
450g (1lb) minced beef
one 396g (14oz) can tomatoes
150ml (¼ pint) beef stock
30ml (2 level tbsp) tomato purée
5ml (1 level tsp) sugar
10ml (2 tsp) chopped fresh oregano or 5ml (1 level tsp) dried oregano
pepper
175g (6oz) lasagne verde
50g (2oz) grated Parmesan cheese

Sauce

25g (1oz) butter
50g (2oz) plain flour
600ml (1 pint) hot milk
pinch of ground nutmeg
salt and pepper
225g (8oz) cottage cheese, sieved

Heat 15ml (1 tbsp) oil in a large pan and fry the onion, garlic and celery until golden. Add the bacon and continue to fry until crisp. Add the minced beef to the pan and fry until browned, stirring constantly. Stir in the tomatoes, stock, tomato purée, sugar, oregano and pepper to taste. Bring to the boil, stirring constantly, then lower the heat, half cover and simmer gently for 20 minutes, until the sauce is well reduced and thickened. Meanwhile to cook the lasagne, bring a large pan of salted water to the boil and stir in a spoonful of oil. Cook the pasta, a few sheets at a time, for 8-10 minutes or until 'al dente' (tender but firm to the bite). Drain and pat dry with a clean tea towel or absorbent kitchen paper. Add more oil to the water for each batch of lasagne. For the sauce, melt the butter in a pan, stir in the flour and cook for 1 minute. Remove the pan from the heat and gradually stir in the milk. Bring to the boil, stirring, add the seasonings and cook for a few minutes until thickened. Remove from the heat, leave to cool slightly, then stir in the cottage cheese. Arrange layers of meat, pasta and sauce in a buttered shallow baking dish, finishing with sauce. Sprinkle the sauce with the Parmesan. Bake in the oven for about 40 minutes, until browned and bubbling. Serve straight from the baking dish.

Oven	Conventional	Fan
Temperature	180°C	160°C
Preheating	Recommended	Not necessary
Shelf position	1st	1st
Time	45 minutes	40 minutes

TOAD IN THE HOLE

Serves 4

450g (1lb) pork sausages
15g (½oz) lard

Batter

125g (4oz) plain flour
2.5ml (½ level tsp) salt
one egg beaten
300ml (½ pint) milk

For the batter, sift the flour and salt into a bowl. Add the egg and a little of the milk. Beat the flour into the liquid, gradually adding the remaining milk to make a smooth batter. Put the sausages and lard into a baking tin measuring about 28 x 18cm (11 x 7 inch). Heat in the oven for 5 minutes, then turn sausages over and return to the oven for 3-4 minutes. Pour the batter into the tin and bake in the oven for about 30 minutes, until well risen and just firm in the centre. Serve immediately with gravy.

Oven	Conventional	Fan
Temperature	200°C	180°C
Preheating	Recommended	Recommended
Shelf position	1st	1st
Time	40-45 minutes	30-35 minutes

CHEESE SOUFFLÉ

Serves 4

25g (1oz) butter	
25g (1oz) flour	
150ml (¼pt) milk	
salt	
freshly milled pepper	
100g (4oz) grated cheddar cheese	
½ level tsp made mustard	
6 large eggs	

Melt the butter in a large saucepan over a low heat. Stir flour into the hot butter and cook over a low heat for 1 minute but do not allow to brown. Gradually stir in the milk, beat well to make a smooth sauce. Bring up to the boil, stirring all the time. At this stage the mixture will be very thick. Cook gently for 1-2 minutes. Draw off the heat and add salt and pepper. Add grated cheese and mustard. Replace over a low heat and stir until cheese has melted. Allow the mixture to cool until the hand can be held against the side of the pan. Crack the eggs, one at a time, placing the whites together in a large basin and beating the yolks thoroughly into the cheese mixture. Whisk the egg whites until just stiff. Using a metal spoon, fold 2 tablespoons of beaten egg whites into cheese sauce. Fold in remaining egg whites. Pour into an ungreased 1 litre (2 pint) soufflé dish. The mixture should fill the dish. Scrape a palette knife over the top of the mixture, smoothing the surface level and sealing the edges against the side of the dish. Bake in the oven for 40-45 minutes. Serve immediately.

Oven	Conventional	Fan
Temperature	190°C	170°C
Preheating	Recommended	Recommended
Shelf position	2nd	1st
Time	45 minutes	40-45 minutes

MOUSSAKA

Serves 4-6

450g (1lb) aubergines, thinly sliced	
about 150ml (¼ pint) vegetable oil	
one large onion, sliced	
one garlic clove, skinned and crushed	
450g (1lb) cooked lamb, minced	
150ml (¼ pint) stock	
5ml (1 level tsp) ground allspice	
30ml (2 tbsp) chopped fresh parsley	
45ml (3 level tbsp) tomato purée	
salt and pepper	
700g (1½lb) potatoes, par boiled and thinly sliced	

Sauce

40g (1½oz) butter	
40g (1½oz) plain flour	
400ml (¾ pint) milk	
good pinch of ground allspice	
one egg, beaten	

Sprinkle the aubergine slices with salt and leave to 'sweat' for about 30-60 minutes. Rinse well in cold water and dry thoroughly. Heat 30ml (2 tbsp) of the oil in a wide frying pan and brown a layer of aubergine slices on both sides. Remove from the pan. Continue browning all the aubergine slices, a single layer at a time and adding more oil to the pan as needed. Then fry the onion and garlic until softened and golden brown. Mix in the lamb, stock, allspice, parsley, tomato purée and seasoning. Arrange layers of aubergine, potato and lamb mixture in the dish, finishing with potato. For the sauce, melt the butter in a saucepan, stir in the flour and cook for 1 minute. Remove the pan from the heat and gradually stir in the milk. Bring to the boil, stirring, and cook for 2-3 minutes until thickened. Add the allspice and seasoning and, when slightly cooled, quickly beat in the egg. Pour the sauce into the dish covering the potatoes. Bake in the oven for about 50 minutes, until the potato is tender and the surface browned.

Oven	Conventional	Fan
Temperature	190°C	170°C
Preheating	Recommended	Not necessary
Shelf position	1st	1st
Time	50-55 minutes	45-50 minutes

CORNISH PASTIES

Makes 6

Filling

450g (1lb) beef, skirt or topside, trimmed
one large onion, finely chopped
125g (4oz) swede or turnip, peeled and finely diced
175g (6oz) potato, peeled and finely diced
salt and pepper
15g (½oz) butter, softened

Pastry

450g (1lb) plain flour
2.5ml (½ level tsp) salt
225g (8oz) block margarine
about 60ml (4 tbsp) cold water

Cut the beef into small pieces. Mix the beef with the onion, swede or turnip, potato, seasoning and butter. For the pastry, sift the flour and salt in a bowl. Rub in the margarine until the mixture resembles fine bread-crumbs. Mix with enough cold water to make a firm dough. Divide into six equal portions and roll out each to a round about 20.5cm (8 inches) in diameter. Divide the filling between the pastry rounds. Damp the edges and seal together on top, crimping the edges. Put on to an oven baking tray. Bake in the oven at the higher temperature for 15-20 minutes, then at the lower temperature for about 40 minutes, until golden brown. Serve hot.

Oven	Conventional	Fan
Temperature	200°C reduce to 180°C	180°C reduce to 160°C
Preheating	Recommended	Recommended
Shelf position	1st	1st
Time	1¼ hours	1 hour

BEEF STUFFED ONIONS

Serves 6

6 even-sized onions, about 175g (6oz) each
30ml (2 tbsp) vegetable oil
50g (2oz) red pepper, deseeded and finely chopped
10ml (2 level tsp) hot Madras curry powder
5ml (1 level tsp) ground cardamom
350g (12oz) minced beef
40g (1½oz) fresh white breadcrumbs
30ml (2 tbsp) chopped fresh parsley
5ml (1 level tsp) salt
pepper

Skin the onions and boil them in a saucepan of salted water for 10 minutes. Drain well, and cut a slice from the top of each. Remove the centre of each, leaving a 'shell' about 1cm (½ inch) thick. Finely chop 50g (2oz) of the scooped-out onion (the rest may be used in another dish). Heat the oil and gently fry the onion for 5 minutes. Add the red pepper with the spices and cook for 2 minutes. Add the minced beef and stir over a moderate heat to brown lightly. Add the breadcrumbs, parsley and seasoning. Spoon the mince mixture into the onion shells. Place in a greased ovenproof dish and cover lightly with foil. Cook in the oven for about 30-40 minutes, until the onions are tender when pierced with a pointed knife. Serve with soured cream spooned over if liked.

Oven	Conventional	Fan
Temperature	190°C	170°C
Preheating	Recommended	Not necessary
Shelf position	1st	1st
Time	40 minutes	30 minutes

Right: Beef Stuffed Onions

STUFFED PEPPERS

Serves 4

4 large red peppers
30ml (2 tbsp) vegetable oil
one small onion, finely chopped
2 garlic cloves, skinned and crushed
125g (4oz) minced beef
125g (4oz) bacon rashers, rinded and chopped
15ml (1 level tbsp) tomato purée
2.5ml (½ level tsp) dried oregano
2.5ml (½ level tsp) dried thyme
2.5ml (½ level tsp) dried basil
30ml (2 tbsp) chopped fresh parsley
10ml (2 tsp) Worcestershire sauce
75g (3oz) long grain rice, cooked
15g (½oz) butter
salt and pepper

Slice off the stalks with some of the pepper to make lids. Remove the seeds and pith, put the peppers into a saucepan of boiling water and boil for 4-5 minutes. Drain them well upside down. Heat the oil in a pan, and fry onion until lightly browned. Mix in the garlic, minced beef and bacon and continue frying and stirring until the beef is coloured. Remove the pan from the heat, stir in the tomato purée, herbs, Worcestershire sauce, rice, butter and seasoning. Fill the peppers with the mixture, stand them upright in an ovenproof dish and place the stalk lids on each. Pour a little hot water into the dish to cover the base. Cover the peppers with foil or a lid. Bake in the oven for about 50-60 minutes, until the peppers are tender.

Oven	Conventional	Fan
Temperature	180°C	160°C
Preheating	Recommended	Not necessary
Shelf position	1st	1st
Time	50-60 minutes	40-50 minutes

BRAISED CELERY

Serves 4

15g (½oz) butter or margarine
15ml (1 tbsp) vegetable oil
one medium onion, chopped
2 large tomatoes, skinned, seeded and chopped
2 medium carrots, peeled and sliced
450ml (¾ pint) stock
bouquet garni
salt and pepper
2 heads of celery, halved lengthways and cleaned
45ml (3 tbsp) chopped fresh parsley

Heat the butter and oil in a flameproof casserole and fry the onion until golden. Mix in the tomatoes, carrots and stock. Add the bouquet garni and seasoning. Press the celery halves into the vegetables. Cover and bake in the oven for about 45-60 minutes, until the celery is tender. Lift the celery with a slotted draining spoon into a serving dish and keep hot. Remove the bouquet garni and boil the vegetables for 2-3 minutes to reduce the liquid if necessary. Process or blend the vegetables, pour over the celery and sprinkle the parsley on top.

Oven	Conventional	Fan
Temperature	170°C	150°C
Preheating	Recommended	Not necessary
Shelf position	1st	1st
Time	45-60 minutes	40-50 minutes

STUFFED AUBERGINES

Serves 4

2 medium aubergines
Stuffing
50g (2oz) cooked ham, chopped
15ml (1 tbsp) chopped fresh parsley
one tomato, skinned and chopped
50g (2oz) fresh breadcrumbs
½ onion, grated
salt and pepper
125g (4oz) grated Cheddar cheese
little stock or beaten egg

Cut the aubergines in half lengthways and scoop out the flesh from the centre of each, leaving 5mm (¼ inch) thick shell. For the stuffing, combine the ham, parsley, tomato, breadcrumbs, onion, seasoning and 50g (2oz) of the cheese with the roughly chopped aubergine flesh. Moisten with a little stock or beaten egg and fill the aubergine shells. Sprinkle with the remaining grated cheese and cover with a lid or foil. Bake in the oven for about 40-45 minutes, until tender. Uncover and cook for a further 10 minutes, until crisp and brown on top. Serve hot with cheese or tomato sauce.

Oven	Conventional	Fan
Temperature	200°C	170°C
Preheating	Recommended	Not necessary
Shelf position	1st	1st
Time	1 hour	50 minutes

CHEESE AND HAM SAVOURY ROLLS
(Käse-Schinken-Röllchen)

Makes 9

One 368g (13oz) packet frozen puff pastry, thawed
125g (4oz) Gouda cheese
125g (4oz) cooked ham, in a thick slice
one egg yolk
one small onion, finely chopped
2.5ml (½ level tsp) black pepper
2.5ml (½ level tsp) oregano
15ml (1 tbsp) finely chopped fresh parsley
one egg, beaten

Roll out the pastry to a square measuring 36 x 36cm (15 x 15 inch), then divide the pastry into nine smaller squares, 13 x 13cm (5 x 5 inch). Cut the cheese and ham into small cubes and mix together with the egg yolk, onion, pepper, oregano and parsley. Spread this mixture over the pastry squares. Brush the edges of each square with beaten egg. Turn the insides of the pastry squares a little, and seal them down well to keep in the filling. Roll up each square of pastry and seal. Lay the rolls, join side down, on a wetted oven baking tray. Brush with egg and bake in the oven for 20-25 minutes, until golden brown.

Oven	Conventional	Fan
Temperature	225°C	200°C
Preheating	Recommended	Recommended
Shelf position	1st	1st
Time	25-30 minutes	20-25 minutes

GRATIN DAUPHINOIS

Serves 4

25g (1oz) butter, softened
1kg (2lb) potatoes, peeled and sliced into thin rings
one large onion, finely chopped
225g (8oz) grated Gruyère cheese
salt and pepper
150ml (¼ pint) single cream

Brush the base and sides of a casserole with some of the butter. Put a layer of potato slices, overlapping, in the bottom of the casserole. Dot with more butter and sprinkle with some of the onion and cheese, and seasoning to taste. Pour over about one-quarter of the cream. Continue with these layers until all the ingredients are used up, finishing with a layer of cheese and pouring the remaining cream over the top. Cover with a lid or buttered greaseproof paper or foil. Bake in the oven for about 50 minutes, until the potatoes are tender when pierced with a skewer. Remove the lid and paper or foil, return to the oven until the surface is browned.

Oven	Conventional	Fan
Temperature	190°C	170°C
Preheating	Recommended	Not necessary
Shelf position	1st	1st
Time	1 hour	50 minutes

MACKEREL IN WINE SAUCE WITH APPLE

Serves 4

four 175g (6oz) mackerel, cleaned
25g (1oz) butter
one medium onion, sliced
25g (1oz) plain flour
150ml (¼ pint) dry white wine
150ml (¼ pint) water
salt and pepper
2 medium Granny Smith apples, cored and thinly sliced (optional)

Arrange the mackerel in a baking dish. Melt the butter in a pan and gently fry the onion until softened and golden. Mix in the flour, gradually add the wine and water, stirring, and cook for 2-3 minutes. Add seasoning to taste. Place the apple slices between the mackerel and pour in the sauce. Cover and bake in the oven for about 40 minutes, until the mackerel flakes easily.

Oven	Conventional	Fan
Temperature	190°C	170°C
Preheating	Not necessary	Not necessary
Shelf position	1st	1st
Time	40-45 minutes	35-40 minutes

FISH SLICE

Serves 4-6

225g (8oz) cooked white fish, flaked
25g (1oz) cooked long grain rice
2 tomatoes, skinned, seeded and chopped
7.5ml (1½ level tsp) curry powder
15ml (1 tbsp) lemon juice
125g (4oz) cream cheese
salt and pepper
450(1lb) prepared puff pastry
one egg, beaten

For the filling, mix together the fish, rice, tomatoes, curry powder, lemon juice, cream cheese and seasoning. Cut the pastry into two portions, one slightly larger than the other. Roll out smaller portion to a rectangle about 18 x 28cm (7 x 11 inch) and place on an oven baking tray. Roll out the larger portion to a rectangle about 1cm (½ inch) larger all round. Fold it in half lengthwise, make straight cuts through the fold to within 2.5cm (1 inch) of the edges. Spread the filling over the pastry base,

brush edges with the beaten egg. Place folded pastry in position over the filling, unfold it carefully to cover the filling and seal the edges well. Brush all over with egg. Bake in the oven at the higher temperature for about 15 minutes, then at the lower temperature for about 15-20 minutes, until well browned. Serve hot or cold.

Oven	Conventional	Fan
Temperature	220°C reduce to 200°C	200°C reduce to 180°C
Preheating	Recommended	Recommended
Shelf position	1st	1st
Time	30-35 minutes	25-30 minutes

HALIBUT CATALAN

Serves 4

90ml (6 tbsp) olive oil
juice of 1 lemon
salt and pepper
4 halibut steaks
one small onion, finely chopped
one garlic clove, skinned and crushed
15ml (1 level tbsp) plain flour
225g (8oz) tomatoes, skinned, seeded and chopped
15ml (1 level tbsp) tomato purée
150ml (¼ pint) dry white wine
150ml (¼ pint) fish stock
45ml (3 tbsp) chopped fresh parsley

Mix together 60ml (4 tbsp) of the oil, the lemon juice and seasoning, and pour into a baking dish. Put the halibut into the dish, marinate for 1-2 hours turning the halibut once. Heat the remaining oil in a frying pan and fry the onion and garlic for 2-3 minutes until golden. Stir in the flour then blend in the tomatoes, purée, wine, stock and seasoning, and simmer for 2-3 minutes. Pour the mixture over the halibut. Cover the dish and bake in the oven for about 40-50 minutes, until the fish flakes easily. Serve hot, sprinkled with the parsley.

Oven	Conventional	Fan
Temperature	180°C	160°C
Preheating	Not necessary	Not necessary
Shelf position	1st	1st
Time	40-50 minutes	30-40 minutes

Left: Mackerel in Wine Sauce with Apple

SAVOURY SUPPERS

FISHERMAN'S PIE

Serves 4

450g (1lb) cod, haddock or coley fillet
300ml (½ pint) milk
salt and pepper
one bay leaf
few parsley sprigs
125g (4oz) shrimps or prawns

Sauce

50g (2oz) butter
one small onion, chopped
one small red pepper, deseeded and chopped
125g (4oz) button mushrooms, wiped and sliced
60ml (4 tbsp) white wine
25g (1oz) plain flour
300ml (½ pint) fish liquor

Topping

700g (1½lb) potatoes, cooked and mashed
25g (1oz) butter, softened
milk, to mix
40g (1½oz) grated cheese

Put the fish into a baking dish. Add the milk, seasoning, bay leaf and parsley. Cover and bake in the oven on the first shelf for about 30 minutes, until the fish flakes easily. Remove the herbs and strain the liquor into a measure. Make this up to 300ml (½ pint) if necessary. Skin and flake the fish, mix together with the shrimps or prawns. For the sauce; melt the butter in a pan and gently fry the onion and pepper until soft but not browned. Mix in the mushrooms and wine, and simmer for 2-3 minutes. Stir in the flour, then gradually stir in the fish cooking liquor. Simmer for 1-2 minutes, stirring. Mix in the fish and place in the pie dish. For the topping, mix together the potatoes, butter, seasoning and enough milk to make the potatoes fairly soft. Fork the potatoes over the fish and cover with the cheese. Bake in the oven on 3rd shelf for about 25 minutes, until the cheese is browned.

Oven	Conventional	Fan
Temperature	180°C	160°C
Preheating	Not necessary	Not necessary
Shelf position	1st and 3rd	1st and 3rd
Time	Fish 35-40 minutes Pie 25-30 minutes	Fish 30-35 minutes Pie 20-25 minutes

SALMON FLAN

Serves 10

Pastry

250g (9oz) plain flour
5ml (1 level tsp) salt
140g (4½oz) block margarine
one egg, beaten

Flan

one 220g (7½oz) can pink salmon, drained, skinned and boned
one 220g (7½oz) can red salmon, drained, skinned and boned
25g (1oz) butter
one medium onion, finely chopped
4 spring onions, trimmed and sliced
50g (2oz) grated cheese
salt and pepper
150ml (¼ pint) single cream
3 eggs
30ml (2 tbsp) lemon juice

For the pastry, sift together the flour and salt into a bowl. Rub in the margarine until the mixture resembles fine breadcrumbs. Stir in the egg and enough water to give a fairly firm dough. Roll out and use to line a 28cm (11 inch) quiche tin. Prick the base lightly, cover with grease-proof paper and fill with baking beans. Bake 'blind' in the oven at the higher temperature for about 20 minutes. Remove the paper and beans during the final 5 minutes cooking time. For the flan, flake all the salmon. Melt the butter in a pan and gently fry the onion and spring onion for about 10 minutes until soft but not browned. Mix together the onions, salmon, cheese and seasoning, then spread evenly in the pastry case. Lightly whisk together the cream, eggs and lemon juice, pour the mixture over the salmon. Bake in the oven at the lower temperature for about 30 minutes until the filling is just set. Serve hot or cold.

Oven	Conventional	Fan
Temperature	200°C reduce to 180°C	180°C reduce to 160°C
Preheating	Recommended	Recommended
Shelf position	1st	1st
Time	Pastry 20 minutes Flan 35-40 minutes	Pastry 15 minutes Flan 30-35 minutes

SAVOURY BAKED FISH FILLETS
(Fisch-Auflauf)
Serves 4

4 pieces of cod or haddock fillet
lemon juice
salt and pepper
one 142g (5oz) can of tomato purée
60g (2½oz) butter
2 small onions, chopped
225g (8oz) mushrooms, wiped and halved
one large gherkin, chopped
2.5 ml (½ level tsp) black pepper
5ml (1 level tsp) thyme
5ml (1 level tsp) basil
125g (4oz) grated cheese
60ml (4 level tbsp) white breadcrumbs

Place the fillets skin side down in a buttered baking dish, sprinkle with lemon juice, salt and pepper. Spread the tomato purée over the four fillets. Melt half of the butter in a pan and fry the onion until beginning to soften. Add the mushrooms and gherkin and fry gently for 2-3 minutes. Season to taste and then spread the mixture over the fillets. Sprinkle over the pepper, thyme and basil. Sprinkle the cheese and breadcrumbs over the fish and dot the remaining butter on the top. Bake in the oven for about 25 minutes, until the fish flakes easily.

Oven	Conventional	Fan
Temperature	200°C	180°C
Preheating	Not necessary	Not necessary
Shelf position	1st	1st
Time	30 minutes	25 minutes

TUNA FISH PIE
Serves 4-6

Pastry
225g (8oz) plain flour
5ml (1 level tsp) salt
50g (2oz) block margarine
50g (2oz) lard
about 60ml (4 tbsp) cold water
milk, to glaze

Filling
25g (1oz) margarine
2 streaky bacon rashers, rinded and chopped
one medium onion, chopped
25g (1oz) plain flour
300ml (½ pint) milk
two 198g (7oz) cans tuna, drained and flaked
3 small pickled cucumbers, chopped
salt and pepper

For the filling, melt the margarine in a pan and fry the bacon and onion until the onion is softened and golden. Mix in the flour, gradually add the milk, stirring, and cook for about 2-3 minutes. Mix in the tuna, pickled cucumber and seasoning. Leave to cool. For the pastry, sift together the flour and salt into a bowl. Rub in the margarine and lard until the mixture resembles fine breadcrumbs. Mix in enough water to give a fairly firm dough. Roll out half the pastry and use to line a 20.5cm (8 inch) pie plate. Roll out the remainder to a round for covering. Spread the filling in the pastry case and damp the edges with milk. Add the pastry top and seal. Crimp the edges and make two slits in the centre for steam to escape. Brush the surface with milk. Bake in the oven for about 30 minutes, until browned on top. Serve hot or cold.

Oven	Conventional	Fan
Temperature	200°C	180°C
Preheating	Recommended	Recommended
Shelf position	1st	1st
Time	30-35 minutes	25-30 minutes

Cakes
Cookies
& Scones

CAKES, COOKIES AND SCONES

VICTORIA SANDWICH CAKE
Makes 6-8 slices

125g (4oz) butter or block margarine
125g (4oz) caster sugar
2 eggs, lightly beaten
125g (4oz) self raising flour, sifted
jam
caster sugar, to dredge

Grease and base line two 18cm (7 inch) sandwich tins. Cream together the butter and sugar in a bowl until pale and fluffy. Gradually beat in the eggs, then fold in the flour using a metal spoon. Divide the mixture between the prepared tins and level the surface. Bake in the oven for about 20 minutes, until well risen, firm to the touch and beginning to shrink away from the sides of the tins. Turn out and cool on a wire rack. When the cakes are cool, sandwich together with jam and dredge with caster sugar.

Oven	Conventional	Fan
Temperature	190°C	160°C
Preheating	Recommended	Not necessary
Shelf position	1st	1st
Time	20 minutes	20-25 minutes

APPLE CAKE
(Apfeltorte)
Makes 8-10 slices

125g (4oz) block margarine
125g (4oz) caster sugar
3 eggs, beaten
5ml (1 tsp) lemon juice
200g (7oz) plain flour
10ml (2 level tsp) baking powder
pinch of salt
30ml (2 tbsp) milk, if necessary
450(1lb) Granny Smith apples, peeled, cored and quartered

Grease a 25.5cm (10 inch) spring-release cake tin. Cream together the margarine and sugar in a bowl until light and fluffy. Gradually beat in the eggs, then the lemon juice. Sift together the flour, baking powder and salt, and fold into the mixture with the milk. Turn the mixture into the prepared tin and level the surface. Cut slits lengthwise in each apple quarter to give a fan appearance. Place core-side down on the mixture. Bake in the oven for about 50 minutes. Turn out and cool on a wire rack, or eat slightly warm.

Oven	Conventional	Fan
Temperature	190°C	170°C
Preheating	Recommended	Not necessary
Shelf position	1st	1st
Time	45-50 minutes	50-60 minutes

APPLECAKE WITH RAISIN FILLING
(Apfeltorte mit Rosinenfullung)
Makes 10-12 slices

450g (1lb) eating apples, peeled and roughly chopped
125g (4oz) seedless raisins
45ml (3 tbsp) rum
200g (7oz) block margarine
250g (9oz) caster sugar
3 eggs, beaten
grated rind of 1 lemon
300g (11oz) plain flour
125g (4oz) cornflour
15ml (3 level tsp) baking powder
50g (2oz) icing sugar and 15-30ml (1-2 tbsp) rum, to ice

Grease a 25.5cm (10 inch) spring release cake tin. Mix together the apples, raisins and rum. Cream together the margarine and sugar in a bowl until light and fluffy. Gradually beat in the egg and lemon rind. Sift in the flours and baking powder, and beat vigorously by hand or use an electric mixer or food processor at high speed for about 1 minute. Turn half of the mixture into the prepared tin and level the surface. Stir the apple mixture and spoon evenly over the mixture in the tin. Layer the remaining cake mixture over the top. Bake in the oven for 1 hour at the higher temperature, then reduce to the lower temperature for about 30-45 minutes, until golden brown. Leave in the tin about 15 minutes then release and cool on a wire rack.

Oven	Conventional	Fan
Temperature	170°C reduce to 150°C	140°C reduce to 130°C
Preheating	Recommended	Not necessary
Shelf position	1st	1st
Time	1½ hours	1¾ hours

CAKES, COOKIES AND SCONES

APRICOT CAKE
(Aprikosenkuchen)

Makes 16-20 slices

200g (7oz) quark
90ml (6 tbsp) milk
150ml (¼ pint) vegetable oil
one size 1 or 2 (large) egg
125g (4oz) caster sugar
1.25ml (¼ level tsp) salt
400g (14oz) plain flour
10ml (2 level tsp) baking powder
three 411g (14½oz) cans apricot halves, well drained
Crumble Topping
200g (7oz) plain flour
125g (4oz) caster sugar
20ml (4 level tsp) vanilla sugar
1.25ml (¼ level tsp) ground cinnamon
125g (4oz) block margarine

Grease an oven baking tray. Beat together the quark, milk, oil, egg, 125g (4oz) sugar and salt in a large bowl. Add 200g (7oz) of the flour and baking powder, and beat again until smooth. Sift the remaining flour on to the work surface. Make a hollow and pour the quark mixture into the centre. Gradually knead the flour into the soft mixture to form a dough. Leave to rest while preparing the crumble. Put the flour, sugars and cinnamon in a bowl. Rub in the margarine by hand in order to achieve a coarse texture – not as fine as that for pastry. Roll out the dough on a lightly floured surface to fit the prepared baking tray. Carefully roll the dough on to the rolling pin and un-roll on to the tray. Arrange the apricots, rounded side uppermost, on the pastry in lines. Sprinkle the crumble between the apricots and around the edge. Bake in the oven for about 35 minutes, until golden brown. When firm enough, cut in slices and cool on a wire rack.

Oven	Conventional	Fan
Temperature	190°C	160°C
Preheating	Recommended	Not necessary
Shelf position	3rd	3rd
Time	25-35 minutes	35-45 minutes

LEMON CREAM
GENOESE SPONGE

Makes 8 slices

40g (1½oz) butter
75g (2½oz) plain flour
15ml (1 level tbsp) cornflour
3 size 1 or 2 (large) eggs, beaten
75g (3oz) caster sugar
Lemon cream
300ml (½ pint) double cream
one 142ml (5 floz) carton soured cream
90ml (6 level tbsp) lemon curd
75g (3oz) shredded coconut, toasted

Grease and base line two 18cm (7 inch) sandwich tins. Heat the butter gently in a saucepan until melted, remove from the heat and allow to stand for a few minutes for the salt and any sediment to settle. Sift together the flour and cornflour. Put the eggs and sugar into a large bowl, resting on a pan of hot water, and whisk until light and creamy; the mixture should be stiff enough to retain the impression of the whisk for a few seconds. Remove from the heat and whisk until cool. Re-sift the flour and carefully fold in half with a metal spoon. Make sure the butter is cooled until it just flows and, taking care not to let the salt and sediment run in, pour the butter around the edges of the mixture. Fold the butter in with the remaining flour. Fold very lightly or the butter will sink and cause a heavy cake. Pour the mixture into the prepared tins. Bake in the oven for about 20 minutes, until golden brown and firm to the touch. Turn out and cool on a wire rack. To decorate, lightly whip the double cream until it just holds its shape. Carefully stir in the soured cream. Split each cake in two and sandwich all together with lemon curd and one-third of the cream mixture. Spread the remaining cream over the top and sides of the cake. Finally, coat the sides with toasted coconut.

Oven	Conventional	Fan
Temperature	190°C	160°C
Preheating	Recommended	Recommended
Shelf position	2nd	1st
Time	20 minutes	25 minutes

CRUMBLE CAKE
(Streuselkuchen)
Makes 16-20 slices

400g (14oz) plain flour
10ml (2 level tsp) baking powder
125g (4oz) caster sugar
20ml (4 level tsp) vanilla sugar
200g (7oz) butter
2 eggs, beaten
5ml (1 tsp) rum essence
200g (7oz) apricot jam

Crumble Topping

200g (7oz) butter
350g (12oz) plain flour
175g (6oz) caster sugar
20ml (4 level tsp) vanilla sugar
7.5ml (1½ level tsp) ground cinnamon

Grease an oven baking tray. Put the flour, baking powder and sugars into a bowl and rub in the butter. Add the egg and rum essence, then knead ingredients together to a smooth dough, using the fingertips. Roll out on a lightly floured surface to about the size of the prepared tray. Carefully roll the pastry on to the rolling pin and un-roll on to the tray. Spread with the apricot jam. For the crumble topping, rub the butter into the flour then add the sugars and cinnamon. Sprinkle the crumble over the jam to give a thickish layer. Bake in the oven for about 40 minutes, until golden brown. When firm enough, cut in slices and cool on a wire rack.

Oven	Conventional	Fan
Temperature	190°C	160°C
Preheating	Recommended	Not necessary
Shelf position	3rd	3rd
Time	30-40 minutes	40-50 minutes

CHOCOLATE AND COFFEE LAYER CAKE
Makes about 16 slices

350g (12oz) soft tub margarine
225g (8oz) caster sugar
50g (2oz) plain chocolate, melted
4 eggs, lightly beaten
225g (8oz) self raising flour, sifted
50g (2oz) cocoa powder, sifted
225g (8oz) icing sugar, sifted
25ml (1½ tbsp) coffee essence
350g (12oz) plain chocolate cake covering
crystallised violets, to decorate

Grease and line a 20.5cm (8 inch) square cake tin. Place 225g (8oz) of the margarine, the caster sugar, melted chocolate, eggs, flour and cocoa in a bowl. Using a wooden spoon, beat for at least 3 minutes until smooth and creamy. Spoon the mixture into the prepared tin and level the surface. Bake in the oven for about 1 hour, until well risen and firm to the touch. Cool in the tin for 5 minutes, then turn out and cool on a wire rack. Meanwhile, cream together the remaining margarine, the icing sugar and coffee essence until light and fluffy. When cold, cut the cake into three layers and sandwich together with the coffee cream. Place on a wire rack standing over a baking tray. In a pan on low hob heat or in a double saucepan melt the cake covering according to the manufacturer's instructions and use to coat the cake completely. Decorate with crystallised violets. Leave to set before placing on a serving plate.

Oven	Conventional	Fan
Temperature	180°C	160°C
Preheating	Recommended	Recommended
Shelf position	1st	1st
Time	1 hour	1¼ hours

FARMHOUSE CAKE

Makes about 16 slices

| 225g (8oz) wholemeal flour |
| 225g (8oz) plain flour |
| 5ml (1 level tsp) ground mixed spice |
| 5ml (1 level tsp) bicarbonate of soda |
| 175g (6oz) butter |
| 225g (8oz) caster sugar |
| 125g (4oz) sultanas |
| 125g (4oz) raisins |
| 45ml (3 tbsp) mixed peel, chopped |
| one egg, lightly beaten |
| 300ml (½ pint) milk |

Line, grease and flour a 20.5cm (8 inch) square cake tin. Sift together the flours, spice and bicarbonate of soda into a bowl. Rub in the butter until the mixture resembles fine breadcrumbs. Stir in the sugar, dried fruit and peel. Make a well in the centre and pour in the egg and some of the milk. Gradually work in the dry ingredients, adding more milk if necessary to give a dropping consistency. Put the mixture into the prepared tin and level the surface. Bake in the oven for about 1¼ hours, until golden brown and firm to the touch. Cover with foil after 1 hour to prevent over-browning. Allow to cool in the tin for 10-15 minutes, then turn out and cool on a wire rack.

Oven	Conventional	Fan
Temperature	170°C	150°C
Preheating	Recommended	Not necessary
Shelf position	1st	1st
Time	1½-1¾ hours	1-1¼ hours

NUT CAKE (Nusskuchen)

Makes 16 slices

| 250g (9oz) block margarine |
| 200g (7oz) caster sugar |
| few drops of almond essence |
| 4 eggs, beaten |
| 250g (9oz) plain flour |
| 15ml (3 level tsp) baking powder |
| 250g (9oz) ground hazelnuts |

Grease two 1kg (2lb) bread tins. Cream together the margarine, sugar and essence in a bowl until light and fluffy. Gradually beat in the eggs. Sift together the flour and baking powder, and fold into the mixture using a metal spoon. Add the hazelnuts. Divide the mixture between the prepared tins and level the surface. Bake in the oven for about 1 hour. Turn out and cool on a wire rack.

Oven	Conventional	Fan
Temperature	170°C	160°C
Preheating	Recommended	Not necessary
Shelf position	1st	1st
Time	50-60 minutes	60-70 minutes

BLACK FOREST GATEAU

Serves 8-10

| 4 eggs, lightly beaten |
| 125g (4oz) caster sugar |
| 75g (3oz) plain flour |
| 25g (1oz) cocoa powder, sifted |
| two 450g (1lb) cans black cherries |
| 60ml (4 tbsp) kirsch |
| 400ml (¾ pint) double cream |
| 125g (4oz) coarsely grated plain chocolate |

Grease and line a 23cm (9 inch) round cake tin, then dust with flour and caster sugar. Put the eggs and sugar into a bowl resting on a saucepan of hot water. Whisk together until the mixture is stiff enough to leave a trail when the whisk is lifted. Remove from the heat and continue whisking until cold. Sift the flour and cocoa over the mixture and fold in lightly. Spread the mixture in the prepared tin. Bake in the oven for about 25 minutes, until well risen and firm to the touch. Turn out and cool on a wire rack. Drain the cherries and mix 75ml (5 tbsp) of the juice with the kirsch. Split the cake into three layers, place a layer on a flat plate and spoon over 45ml (3 tbsp) of the cherry syrup. Whisk the cream until stiff and spread some thinly over the sponge layer. Reserve a few cherries for decoration and scatter half the remainder over the cream. Repeat the layers of sponge, syrup, cream and cherries, finishing with the third cake round. Spoon over the remaining syrup. Fill a piping bag fitted with a large star nozzle with the remaining cream and pipe whirls of cream around the edge of the cake. Decorate with the reserved cherries and fill the centre of the gâteau with the grated chocolate.

Oven	Conventional	Fan
Temperature	180°C	160°C
Preheating	Recommended	Recommended
Shelf position	1st	1st
Time	30 minutes	25 minutes

Black Forest Gâteau

CAKES, COOKIES AND SCONES

CHRISTMAS CAKE

225g (8oz) currants
225g (8oz) sultanas
225g (8oz) raisins, chopped
125g (4oz) mixed peel, chopped
125g (4oz) glâcé cherries, halved
50g (2oz) nibbed almonds
225g (8oz) plain flour
pinch of salt
2.5ml (½ level tsp) ground mace
2.5ml (½ level tsp) ground cinnamon
225g (8oz) butter
225g (8oz) soft dark brown sugar
grated rind of 1 lemon
4 eggs, lightly beaten
30ml (2 tbsp) brandy

Grease and line a 20.5cm (8 inch) round cake tin, using two thicknesses of greaseproof paper. Tie a double band of brown paper around the outside. Mix together the fruits and nuts. Sift the flour, salt and spices. Cream together the butter, sugar and lemon rind in a bowl until pale and fluffy. Gradually beat in the eggs. Fold in half the flour using a metal spoon. Mix the remaining flour with the fruit and gently fold into the mixture with the brandy. Turn the mixture into the prepared tin and smooth the surface, making a slight dip in the centre. Bake in the oven for about 1½ hours, then cover the top of the cake with several thicknesses of greaseproof paper to avoid over-browning; continue to cook for the remaining time or until a warmed skewer inserted into the centre comes out clean. When cooked, cool the cake in the tin, then turn out on to a wire rack.

Oven	Conventional	Fan
Temperature	150°C	130°C
Preheating	Recommended	Not necessary
Shelf position	1st	1st
Time	3½ hours	3-3¼ hours

Almond Paste

175g (6oz) icing sugar
175g (6oz) caster sugar
350g (12oz) ground almonds
2.5ml (½ tsp) vanilla flavouring
one or two size 6 (small) eggs, beaten
lemon juice
sieved apricot jam, to brush

Sift the icing sugar into a bowl and mix with the caster sugar and almonds. Add the vanilla with sufficient egg and lemon juice to mix to a stiff dough. Form into a ball and knead lightly. This makes 700g (1½lb) almond paste. To apply almond paste, trim the top of the cake if necessary. Measure round the cake with a piece of string. Brush the sides of the cake generously with sieved apricot jam. Take half the almond paste and form into a roll. Dredge the working surface generously with icing sugar and roll out the almond paste as long as the string and as wide as the cake is deep. Press the strip firmly on to the sides of the cake, smoothing the join with a round bladed knife and keeping the edges square. Brush the top of the cake with jam. Roll out the remaining almond paste into a round to fit the top of the cake. Turn the cake upside down, centring it exactly on the paste, and press down firmly. Smooth the join, loosen the paste from the board and turn the cake the right way up. Check that the top edge is level. Leave for 2-3 days before coating with royal icing.

Royal Icing

700g (1½lb) icing sugar
3 egg whites

Sift the icing sugar twice. Place the egg whites in a bowl and stir lightly, just to break them up. Add half the icing sugar and stir until well mixed, using a wooden spoon. Beat for 5-10 minutes, until the icing is smooth and glossy. Gradually add the remaining icing sugar, beating until the icing forms stiff peaks when pulled with the spoon. Cover with a damp cloth or polythene to prevent the icing drying out. To rough ice the cake, spoon the icing on top of the cake and smooth it with a palette knife to cover the top and sides evenly. Draw the icing up into peaks as liked. Put on any decorations before the icing is completely set.

YORKSHIRE PARKIN

Makes about 16 slices

225g (8oz) plain flour
5ml (1 level tsp) bicarbonate of soda
2.5ml (½ level tsp) ground mixed spice
pinch of salt
125g (4oz) medium oatmeal
125g (4oz) butter
175g (6oz) soft dark brown sugar
125g (4oz) golden syrup
150ml (¼ pint) milk

Grease and base line a 20.5cm (8 inch) square cake tin. Sift together the flour, bicarbonate of soda, mixed spice and salt into a bowl. Stir in the oatmeal. Melt the butter, sugar and syrup in a saucepan over a low heat.

CAKES, COOKIES AND SCONES

Make a well in the centre of the dry ingredients, pour in the syrup mixture and milk, and mix thoroughly. Pour the mixture into the prepared tin. Bake in the oven for about 40 minutes, until well risen and firm to the touch. Turn out and cool on a wire rack. Store in an airtight container for 2-3 days before serving.

Oven	Conventional	Fan
Temperature	180°C	160°C
Preheating	Recommended	Not necessary
Shelf position	1st	1st
Time	45 minutes	40 a inutes

GINGER NUTS
Makes about 18

125g (4oz) self raising flour
2.5ml (½ level tsp) bicarbonate of soda
10ml (2 level tsp) ground ginger
pinch of ground cinnamon
10ml (2 level tsp) caster sugar
50g (2oz) butter · 75g (3oz) golden syrup

Well grease two oven baking trays. Sift together the flour, bicarbonate of soda, ginger, cinnamon and sugar into a bowl. Melt the butter in a pan and stir in the syrup. Stir the syrup mixture into the dry ingredients and mix well. Roll the dough into small balls the size of a walnut, place well apart on the prepared trays and flatten slightly. Bake in the oven for about 7 minutes. Cool for a few minutes, then lift on to a wire rack to cool. Store in an airtight tin.

Oven	Conventional	Fan
Temperature	190°C	170°C
Preheating	Recommended	Recommended
Shelf position	1st and 2nd	1st and 3rd
Time	12 minutes	7 minutes

CHERRY GARLANDS
Makes 24

225g (8oz) soft tub margarine
50g (2oz) icing sugar, sifted · 200g (7oz) plain flour
150g (5oz) cornflour · vanilla flavouring
50g (2oz) glâcé cherries, very finely chopped
quartered cherries and angelica, to decorate
icing sugar to dredge

Grease two oven baking trays. Cream together the margarine and icing sugar in a bowl until pale and fluffy. Sift in the flours, with a few drops of vanilla and the chopped cherries. If using an electric hand mixer, beat for 3-4 minutes. By hand, beat until the mixture is very soft.

Spoon half the mixture into a piping bag fitted with a 1cm (½ inch) star nozzle. Pipe 5cm (2 inch) rings on to the prepared baking trays, allowing room for spreading. Decorate with a quartered cherry and pieces of angelica. Repeat with the remaining mixture. Bake in the oven for about 15 minutes, until pale golden, reversing the trays if necessary. Allow to firm up slightly on the baking trays for about 30 seconds, then slide on to a wire rack to cool. Dredge with icing sugar. Store in an airtight container for up to 2-3 weeks.

Oven	Conventional	Fan
Temperature	190°C	170°C
Preheating	Recommended	Recommended
Shelf position	1st and 4th	1st and 3rd
Time	15-18 minutes	12-15 minutes

SPICED CARROT CAKE
Makes 6-8 slices

450g (1lb) plain wholemeal flour
large pinch of salt
2.5ml (½ level tsp) bicarbonate of soda
15ml (1 level tbsp) ground cinnamon
2.5ml (½ level tsp) ground nutmeg
1.25ml (¼ level tsp) ground cloves
125g (4oz) butter
450g (1lb) carrots, peeled and coarsely grated
125g (4oz) dark brown soft sugar
75g (3oz) clear honey
75g (3oz) black treacle
30ml (2 tbsp) milk
30ml (2 level tbsp) demerara sugar

Grease and line a 20.5cm (8 inch) round cake tin. Sift together the flour, salt, bicarbonate of soda and spices into a large bowl. Rub in the butter. Add the grated carrots, then make a well in the centre. Warm together the sugar, honey and treacle in a pan over a low heat, and pour into the dry ingredients. Mix to a stiff dropping consistency with the milk. Turn the mixture into the prepared tin. Level the surface and sprinkle over the demerara sugar. Bake in the oven for about 1 hour, until a fine, warmed skewer inserted in the centre of the cake comes out clean. Turn out and cool on a wire rack.

Oven	Conventional	Fan
Temperature	190°C	170°C
Preheating	Recommended	Not necessary
Shelf position	1st	1st
Time	1-1¼ hours	1 hour

COCONUT FLAPJACKS
Makes 16

| 125g (4oz) demerara sugar |
| 125g (4oz) butter or block margarine |
| 60ml (4 level tbsp) golden syrup |
| 175g (6oz) porridge oats |
| 50g (2oz) desiccated coconut |

Grease a 20.5cm (8 inch) shallow square cake tin. Put the sugar, butter and golden syrup in a saucepan and heat gently until melted. Remove from the heat and stir in the oats and coconut. Press the mixture into the prepared tin. Bake in the oven for about 20 minutes, until golden and firm to the touch. Cool for 5 minutes, then cut into squares. Cool completely before removing from the tin.

Oven	Conventional	Fan
Temperature	180°C	160°C
Preheating	Recommended	Recommended
Shelf position	1st	1st
Time	25 minutes	20 minutes

BROWNIES
Makes 16

| 125g (4oz) butter or block margarine |
| 125g (4oz) plain chocolate, broken in squares |
| 125g (4oz) soft dark brown sugar |
| 125g (4oz) self raising flour |
| pinch of salt |
| 2 eggs, lightly beaten |
| 75g (3oz) walnuts, roughly chopped |
| 15-30ml (1-2 tbsp) milk |

Grease and base line a 20.5cm (8 inch) square cake tin. Melt the butter and chocolate in a bowl resting on a saucepan of hot water. Remove the bowl from the heat and stir in the sugar. Leave to cool. Sift together the flour and salt into a bowl, make a well in the centre and pour in the cooled chocolate mixture. Mix together then beat in the eggs and walnuts, adding enough milk to make a soft dropping consistency. Pour the mixture into the prepared tin. Bake in the oven for about 30 minutes, until a skewer inserted into the centre comes out clean. Cool in the tin before cutting into sixteen squares.

Oven	Conventional	Fan
Temperature	180°C	160°C
Preheating	Recommended	Recommended
Shelf position	1st	1st
Time	30 minutes	25-30 minutes

BANANA TEABREAD
Makes 8 slices

| 450g (1lb) bananas, peeled |
| 225g (8oz) self raising flour |
| 2.5ml (½ level tsp) salt |
| 1.25ml (¼ level tsp) ground nutmeg |
| 125g (4oz) butter or block margarine |
| 125g (4oz) caster sugar |
| grated rind of 1 lemon |
| 2 large eggs |
| 120ml (8 level tbsp) thick honey |
| 8 sugar lumps |

Grease and base line a 1.7 litre (3 pint) loaf tin. Mash the banana flesh using a fork or potato masher. Sift into a bowl the flour, salt and nutmeg. Rub in the butter until the mixture resembles fine breadcrumbs. Stir in the sugar, lemon rind, eggs, 90ml (6 level tbsp) of the honey and mashed banana. Beat well until evenly mixed. Spoon the mixture into the prepared tin. Bake in the oven for about 1¼ hours, covering lightly if necessary. Test with a fine skewer which should come out clean when the teabread is cooked. Cool slightly, then turn out and cool on a wire rack. Gently warm the remaining honey and brush over the teabread. Roughly crush the sugar lumps and scatter over the surface. Serve sliced, buttered if wished.

Oven	Conventional	Fan
Temperature	180°C	160°C
Preheating	Recommended	Not necessary
Shelf position	1st	1st
Time	About 1½ hours	About 1¼ hours

Left: Spiced Carrot Cake, Coconut Flapjacks and Brownies

CAKES, COOKIES AND SCONES

PEANUT SABLES

Makes 16-30

125g (4oz) butter
175g (6oz) plain flour
125g (4oz) grated Red Leicester or mature Cheddar cheese
salt and pepper
pinch of cayenne
15-30ml (1-2 tbsp) water
one egg, beaten
50g (2oz) salted peanuts, chopped

Grease an oven baking tray. Rub the butter into the flour in a bowl. Add the cheese. Stir well and add the seasonings. Bind to a firm dough with the water and knead lightly. Roll out to a 20.5cm (8inch) square and trim the edges to neaten. Place on the prepared baking tray, cut into four strips, spaced apart. Brush with beaten egg and press in the peanuts. Cut the strips into sixteen squares or thirty two small triangles, and separate them. Bake in the oven for about 20 minutes, until well browned. Cool on wire racks.

Oven	Conventional	Fan
Temperature	180°C	160°C
Preheating	Recommended	Recommended
Shelf position	1st	1st
Time	20-25 minutes	15-20 minutes

MERINGUES

Makes 12-16 meringue shells

2 egg whites
125g (4oz) caster sugar
150ml (¼ pint) whipped cream

Line an oven baking tray with silicone (non-stick) paper. Put the egg whites into a grease-free bowl. Whisk until stiff and holding sharp peaks. Whisk in half the sugar, sprinkling in about 10ml (2 level tsp) at a time. Lightly fold in the remaining sugar. Pipe through a piping bag fitted with a large nozzle or shape into ovals with a dessert spoon on to the prepared baking tray. Dry out in the oven for 3 hours, until the meringues are firm and crisp but still white. Cool on a wire rack. Store in an airtight container. Sandwich them together with the whipped cream.

Oven	Conventional	Fan
Temperature	80°C	60°C
Preheating	Recommended	Not necessary
Shelf position	1st	1st
Time	3 hours	3 hours

EVERDAY GINGERBREAD

Makes about 16 slices

450g (1lb) plain flour · 5ml (1 level tsp) salt
15ml (1 level tbsp) ground ginger
5ml (1 level tsp) baking powder
5ml (1 level tsp) bicarbonate of soda
175g (6oz) butter or block margarine
225g (8oz) demerara sugar
175g (6oz) treacle · 175g (6oz) golden syrup
300ml (½ pint) milk · one egg, lightly beaten

Grease and base line a 23cm (9 inch) square cake tin. Sift together the flour, salt, ginger, baking powder and bicarbonate of soda into a bowl. Melt the butter, sugar, treacle and syrup in a saucepan over a low heat. Mix in the milk and egg. Make a well in the centre of the dry ingredients, pour in the liquid and mix thoroughly. Pour the mixture into the prepared tin. Bake in the oven for about 1¼ hours, until well risen and firm to the touch. Turn out and cool on a wire rack.

Oven	Conventional	Fan
Temperature	170°C	140°C
Preheating	Recommended	Not necessary
Shelf position	1st	1st
Time	1¼ hours	1¼ hours

ALMOND MACAROONS

Makes 10

one egg white
50g (2oz) ground almonds
100g (3¼oz) caster sugar
2.5ml (½ tsp) almond essence · a few split almonds
a little egg white, to glaze

Line 1-2 oven baking trays with silicone (non-stick) paper or rice paper. Whisk the egg white until stiff and fold in the ground almonds, caster sugar and almond essence. Place spoonfuls of the mixture on the baking trays, leaving plenty of room for spreading. (Alternatively, pipe the mixture on to the paper, using a piping bag fitted with a 1cm (½ inch) plain nozzle). Top each macaroon with a split almond and brush with egg white. Bake in the oven for about 12 minutes, until just beginning to colour. Cool on a wire rack.

Oven	Conventional	Fan
Temperature	180°C	160°C
Preheating	Recommended	Recommended
Shelf position	1st	1st
Time	15-18 minutes	10-12 minutes

VIENNA APPLE SLICES
(Wiener Apfelschnitten)

Makes 16-20 squares

| 200g (7oz) block margarine |
| 200g (7oz) caster sugar |
| 3 eggs, beaten |
| grated rind of 1 lemon |
| 300g (11oz) plain flour |
| 125g (4oz) cornflour |
| 10ml (2 level tsp) baking powder |
| 450g (1lb) eating apples, peeled and thinly sliced |
| 30ml (2 tbsp) rum |
| 75ml (5 level tbsp) apricot jam, warmed |
| 50g (2oz) flaked almonds |

Grease the oven baking tray. Cream together the margarine and caster sugar until light and fluffy. Gradually beat in the eggs and lemon rind. Sift in the flours and baking powder, and mix with an electric mixer at high speed or vigorously by hand for about 1 minute. Fold the apple slices into the mixture with the rum. Spread the mixture over the prepared tray. Bake in the oven for about 40 minutes. While still warm, spread with the apricot jam and scatter the almonds over. When firm enough, cut into squares or fingers and cool on a wire rack.

Oven	Conventional	Fan
Temperature	190°C	170°C
Preheating	Recommended	Not necessary
Shelf position	3rd	3rd
Time	40 minutes	35-40 minutes

ROCK BUNS

Makes 12

| 125g (4oz) butter or block margarine |
| 225g (8oz) plain flour |
| 10ml (2 level tsp) baking powder |
| pinch of salt |
| 2.5ml (½ level tsp) ground mixed spice |
| grated rind of ½ lemon |
| 125g (4oz) demerara sugar |
| 125g (4oz) mixed dried fruit |
| one egg, lightly beaten |
| 10ml (2 tsp) milk |

Thoroughly grease an oven baking tray. Sift together the flour, baking powder, salt and spice into a bowl. Rub in the butter until the mixture resembles fine bread-crumbs. Stir in the lemon rind, sugar and fruit. Make a

well in the centre and pour in the egg. Bind together loosely using a fork and adding milk if necessary to make a firm dough. Do not overmix. Use two forks to shape the mixture into twelve rough heaps on the baking tray. Bake in the oven for about 18 minutes, until golden brown.

Oven	Conventional	Fan
Temperature	200°C	180°C
Preheating	Recommended	Recommended
Shelf position	1st	1st
Time	18-20 minutes	15-18 minutes

PRUNE AND NUT TEABREAD

Makes 8-10 slices

| 275g (10oz) self raising flour |
| 7.5ml (1½ level tsp) ground cinnamon |
| pinch of salt |
| 75g (3oz) butter or block margarine |
| 75g (3oz) demerara sugar |
| one egg, beaten |
| 100ml (4floz) milk |
| 50g (2oz) walnuts, chopped |
| 125g (4oz) stoned, tenderised prunes |

Grease, base line and grease a 1.3 litre (2¼ pint) shallow loaf tin. Combine flour, cinnamon and salt in a bowl. Rub in the butter. Stir in the sugar, and make a well in the centre. Add the egg and milk, and mix to form a smooth dough. Using floured hands, shape the mixture into sixteen even-sized balls. Place eight in the base of the tin. Sprinkle over half the nuts and snip over all the prune flesh. Place the remaining balls on top and sprinkle over remaining nuts. Bake in the oven for about 40 minutes, until firm to the touch, covering lightly if necessary. Turn out and cool on a wire rack. Wrap and leave for one or two days to mature before slicing and buttering.

Oven	Conventional	Fan
Temperature	190°C	170°C
Preheating	Recommended	Not necessary
Shelf position	1st	1st
Time	50 minutes	40-45 minutes

CAKES, COOKIES AND SCONES

QUICK WHITE LOAF AND ROLLS

Makes 2 loaves

15g (½oz) fresh yeast or 7.5ml (1½ level tsp) dried yeast and 5ml (1 level tsp) sugar
about 300ml (½ pint) tepid water
450(1lb) strong plain flour
5ml (1 level tsp) salt

Grease two 450(1lb) loaf tins. Blend the fresh yeast with the water, or stir the sugar into the water, whisk in the dried yeast and leave in a warm place for about 10 minutes until frothy. Sift together the flour and salt into bowl. Make a well in the centre and gradually add the yeast liquid. Mix to an elastic dough, adding more water if necessary. Turn the dough on to a floured surface and knead for about 10 minutes until really smooth. Divide the dough into two portions, shape and put into the prepared tins. Cover with oiled cling film and allow to rise in a warm place for about 1 hour, until the dough fills the tins and springs back when lightly pressed. Bake in the oven for about 35 minutes, until the loaves are golden brown and sound hollow when rapped with the knuckles. Turn out and cool on a wire rack.

Bread rolls: Shape 50g (2oz) portions of dough. Rise to double size on greased oven baking tray. Bake 15-20 minutes.

Oven	Conventional	Fan
Temperature	230°C	210°C
Preheating	Recommended	Recommended
Shelf position	1st	1st
Time	40 minutes	35 minutes

WHOLEMEAL BREAD

15g (½oz) fresh yeast or 15ml (3 level tsp) dried yeast and 5ml (1 level tsp) sugar
about 300ml (½ pint) tepid water
450(1lb) wholemeal flour
5ml (1 level tsp) salt

Mix together the flour and salt in a warm mixing bowl. Cream the fresh yeast with a little of the water, or stir the sugar into the water, whisk in the dried yeast and leave in a warm place for 10 minutes until frothy. Make a well in the centre of the flour and gradually add the yeast and liquid. Using a palette knife, work the flour and yeast liquid together. Turn out on to a lightly floured surface and knead for about 10 minutes, until a soft pliable dough is formed. Return the dough to a clean mixing bowl, cover with oiled cling film and leave to

rise in a warm place for about 1½ hours, until doubled in size. Meanwhile, grease two 1kg (2lb) loaf tins. Turn the dough on to a floured surface and knead for a further 2 minutes. Shape the dough and place in the prepared tins. Cover with oiled cling film and leave to rise in a warm place for about 45 minutes, until the dough reaches the top of the tins. Bake in the oven at the higher temperature for about 20 minutes, then at the lower temperature for the remainder of the time, until the bread sounds hollow when rapped with the knuckles. Turn out and cool on a wire rack.

Oven	Conventional	Fan
Temperature	250°C reduce to 230°C	230°C reduce to 210°C
Preheating	Recommended	Recommended
Shelf position	1st	1st
Time	40 minutes	30-35 minutes

BROWN SODA BREAD

225g (8oz) strong plain white flour
225g (8oz) strong plain wholemeal flour
15ml (3 level tsp) salt
15ml (3 level tsp) bicarbonate of soda
15ml (3 level tsp) cream of tartar
150ml (¼ pint) milk
150ml (¼ pint) water
15ml (1 level tbsp) golden syrup
5ml (1 tsp) vinegar

Grease an oven baking tray. Sift together the flours, salt, bicarbonate of soda and cream of tartar into a bowl. Mix together the milk, water, syrup and vinegar. Make a well in the centre of the flour and pour in the liquid. Mix to a fairly stiff dough with the blade of a knife. Knead lightly then shape into a flat round about 5cm (2 inches) deep. Make a deep cross in the top with a sharp knife. Place on the prepared baking tray. Bake in the oven at the higher temperature for 15 minutes, then at the lower temperature for the remaining time, until well risen and golden brown. Cool on a wire rack.

Oven	Conventional	Fan
Temperature	220°C reduce to 200°C	200°C reduce to 180°C
Preheating	Recommended	Recommended
Shelf position	1st	1st
Time	30 minutes	25 minutes

Right: Quick White Loaf, Rolls and Wholemeal Bread

110

NUT RING
(Nusskranz)

Makes 10-12 slices

| 300g (11oz) plain flour |
| 10ml (2 level tsp) baking powder |
| 150g (5oz) block margarine |
| 125g (4oz) caster sugar |
| 20ml (4 level tsp) vanilla sugar |
| one egg |
| one egg yolk |

Filling

| 200g (7oz) ground hazelnuts |
| 125g (4oz) caster sugar |
| one egg, beaten |
| few drops of almond essence |

Grease an oven baking tray. Sift together the flour and baking powder into a bowl. Rub in the margarine. Add the sugars. Work in the whole egg and egg yolk, then knead the mixture into a dough. Wrap in cling film and chill for 20 minutes. Roll out into a rectangle about 5mm (¼ inch) in thickness. For the filling, combine together the hazelnuts, sugar, some of the egg and almond essence. Spread evenly over the rolled out dough. Roll up from a long side into a Swiss roll shape. Ease the roll into a ring on the prepared baking tray, and pinch the ends together. Brush evenly with beaten egg. Bake in the oven for about 40 minutes. Cool on a wire rack.

Oven	Conventional	Fan
Temperature	180°C	160°C
Preheating	Recommended	Not necessary
Shelf position	2nd	2nd
Time	35-40 minutes	40-50 minutes

DATE BUTTER COOKIES

Makes 24

| 75g (3oz) butter |
| 225g (8oz) self-raising flour |
| pinch of salt |
| 2.5ml (½ level tsp) baking powder |
| 125g (4oz) caster sugar |
| 125g (4oz) dates, chopped |
| one egg, beaten |

Well grease a Swiss roll tin 28.9 x 18.9cm (11⅜ x 7⅜ inch). Sift together the flour, salt and baking powder into a bowl. Rub in the butter. Stir in the sugar and dates, bind the mixture together with the egg. Knead lightly and press into the prepared tin. Bake in the oven for about 20 minutes until well browned. While warm cut into twenty-four fingers. Cool in the tin, then invert carefully on to a wire rack. Leave until cold. Store in an airtight container for up to 3 weeks.

Oven	Conventional	Fan
Temperature	190°C	170°C
Preheating	Recommended	Recommended
Shelf position	1st	1st
Time	20-25 minutes	18-20 minutes

BUTTER SHORTBREAD

Makes 8 pieces

| 175g (6oz) plain flour |
| pinch of salt |
| 50g (2oz) caster sugar |
| 125g (4oz) butter |
| caster sugar to dredge |

Grease an oven baking tray and place an 18cm (7 inch) fluted flan ring on it. Sift together the flour and salt into a bowl. Stir in the caster sugar. Work in the butter then knead lightly to bind the dough together. Press in to the flan ring and prick evenly with a fork. Bake in the oven for about 40 minutes until a light golden brown. Lift off the flan ring, sprinkle shortbread with caster sugar and mark while warm into 8 portions with a knife. When cool, cut into pieces and place on a wire rack until completely cold. Store in an airtight container.

Oven	Conventional	Fan
Temperature	170°C	150°C
Preheating	Recommended	Recommended
Shelf position	2nd	2nd
Time	40-45 minutes	40-45 minutes

CAKES, COOKIES AND SCONES

CHELSEA BUNS

Makes 9

225g (8oz) strong white flour
15g (½oz) fresh yeast or 7.5ml (1½ level tsp) dried yeast
100ml (4floz) tepid milk
2.5ml (½ level tsp) salt
15g (½oz) butter
one size 4 egg, lightly beaten
melted butter, to brush
75g (3oz) mixed dried fruit
30ml (2tbsp) mixed peel, chopped
50g (2oz) soft light brown sugar
clear honey, to glaze

Grease an 18cm (7 inch) square cake tin. Put 50g (2oz) of the flour in a large bowl and blend together with the yeast and milk until smooth. Set aside for about 10-20 minutes in a warm place, until the batter froths. Sift together the remaining flour and the salt into a bowl. Rub in the butter. Mix, then beat into the batter with the egg to give a fairly soft dough that leaves the sides of the bowl clean. Turn out on to a lightly floured surface and knead until smooth. Put into a clean bowl, cover with oiled cling film and leave to rise for about 1-1½ hours, until doubled in size. Knead the dough thoroughly and roll out into an oblong, 30.5 x 23cm (12 x 9 inch). Brush with melted butter and sprinkle with the dried fruit, peel and brown sugar. Roll up from the longest side and seal the edges with water. Cut into nine slices and place cut sides down in the prepared tin. Cover with oiled cling film and leave to rise for about 45 minutes, until doubled in size. Bake in the oven for about 25 minutes, until golden brown. Brush with the honey while still hot. Cool on a wire rack.

Oven	Conventional	Fan
Temperature	190°C	160°C
Preheating	Recommended	Recommended
Shelf position	1st	1st
Time	25 minutes	20-25 minutes

HOT CROSS BUNS

Makes 12

450g (1lb) strong white flour
5ml (1 level tsp) salt
5ml (1 level tsp) ground mixed spice
5ml (1 level tsp) ground nutmeg
125g (4oz) caster sugar
50g (2oz) butter or block margarine
20g (¾oz) fresh yeast or 20ml (4 level tsp) dried yeast and 5ml (1 level tsp) sugar
about 300ml (½ pint) tepid milk or milk and water
50g (2oz) currants
50g (2oz) mixed peel, chopped

Grease two oven baking trays. Sift together the flour, salt and spices into a bowl. Stir in 50g (2oz) of the caster sugar and rub in the butter. Blend the fresh yeast with the liquid, or stir the sugar into the liquid, whisk in the dried yeast and leave in a warm place for about 10 minutes until frothy. Make a well in the centre of the flour and pour in the yeast liquid. Mix to an elastic dough. Turn the dough on to a lightly floured surface and knead for about 10 minutes, until really smooth. Put in a clean bowl, cover with oiled cling film and leave to rise for 1-1½ hours, until doubled in size. Knead in the currants and peel until evenly distributed. Form the dough into a long roll and cut into twelve equal slices. Shape each into a bun, place on the prepared baking trays and mark with a cross. Cover with oiled cling film and leave to rise for about 45 minutes, until doubled in size. Bake in the oven for about 20 minutes, until the buns are golden brown and sound hollow when rapped with the knuckles. Meanwhile, dissolve the remaining caster sugar in 30ml (2 tbsp) water. Brush the hot buns with the glaze and cool on a wire rack.

Oven	Conventional	Fan
Temperature	190°C	160°C
Preheating	Recommended	Recommended
Shelf position	1st	1st
Time	25 minutes	20-25 minutes

Puddings Hot & Cold

Rice Pudding

PUDDINGS

RICE PUDDING

Serves 4

| 40g (1½oz) pudding rice |
| 25g (1oz) sugar |
| 600ml (1 pint) milk |
| 15g (½oz) butter |
| one cinnamon stick or |
| 2.5ml (½ level tsp) ground nutmeg |

Generously butter a 900ml (1½ pint) ovenproof dish. Place the rice and sugar in the dish. Pour in the milk and add the butter and cinnamon, or sprinkle with the nutmeg. Bake in the oven for about 10 minutes at the higher temperature or until the pudding is bubbling and a skin is beginning to form. Reduce to the lower temperature and cook for the remaining time, or until the rice is soft and creamy and the skin golden in colour. Remove the cinnamon stick if used and serve hot.

Oven	Conventional	Fan
Temperature	230°C reduce to 150°C	210°C reduce to 130°C
Preheating	Recommended	Not necessary
Shelf position	1st	1st
Time	2 hours	2 hours

TIPSY FRUIT COMPOTE

Serves 8

| 275g (10oz) dried prunes, soaked overnight |
| 275g (10oz) dried apricots, soaked overnight |
| 50g (2oz) sultanas, soaked overnight |
| 75g (3oz) dried apple rings, soaked overnight |
| one cinnamon stick |
| 60ml (4 tbsp) whisky |
| 600ml (1 pint) unsweetened orange juice |
| 15ml (1 level tbsp) soft brown sugar |
| thinly pared rind of 1 lemon, cut into fine shreds |
| 3 bananas, peeled and sliced |

Drain the soaked fruit and place in an ovenproof dish with the cinnamon stick. Combine the whisky, orange juice, sugar and lemon rind. Pour over the fruit. Cover with foil and bake in the oven for about 25 minutes, or until the fruit is tender. Leave to cool. Add the sliced bananas before serving. Serve warm or cold.

Oven	Conventional	Fan
Temperature	180°C	160°C
Preheating	Not necessary	Not necessary
Shelf position	1st	1st
Time	30 minutes.	25 minutes

PEACH AND BLACKCURRANT CHARLOTTE

Serves 4

| 6 large slices of bread, medium cut |
| 50g (2oz) butter |
| 700g (1½lb) fresh peaches, halved and stoned |
| 30ml (2 tbsp) water |
| 225g (8oz) blackcurrants |
| 1.25ml (¼ level tsp) ground cinnamon |
| 150g (5oz) sugar |
| 25g (1oz) fresh white breadcrumbs |

Remove the crusts from the bread, keep one slice for the base of the tin and cut each of the remainder into three fingers. Melt the butter, dip in the large bread slice and place butter side down in a 12.5cm (5 inch) Charlotte or cake tin. Dip all the smaller pieces into the butter and press them firmly butter side out against the inside edge of the tin, keeping back some pieces to cover the top later. Cut the peaches into thickish slices and put them into a pan with the water. Cook until the peaches begin to soften. Add the blackcurrants, cinnamon, sugar and breadcrumbs. Put the warm fruit into the bread lined tin and place remaining bread on top to cover the fruit. Bake in the oven for about 50 minutes, until the surface bread is crisp and brown. Leave in the tin for 5 minutes to settle, then invert carefully on to a serving dish. Alternatively leave in the tin until cold. Serve hot or cold with cream or custard.

Oven	Conventional	Fan
Temperature	180°C	160°C
Preheating	Recommended	Not necessary
Shelf position	1st	1st
Time	55-60 minutes	50-55 minutes

PUDDINGS

GOLDEN SYRUP ROLL

Serves 8

275g (10oz) self raising flour
150g (5oz) shredded suet
75g (3oz) demerara sugar
one egg
about 150ml (¼ pint) milk
50g (2oz) fresh white breadcrumbs
225g (8oz) golden syrup

Put the flour, suet and 50g (2oz) of the sugar into a bowl and mix well together. Whisk the egg and milk together, add to the flour mixture and bind to a firm dough. Roll out the dough to an oblong about 38 x 30.5cm (15 x 12 inch). Scatter over the crumbs to within 2.5cm (1 inch) of the edges. Spoon the golden syrup over the crumbs. Fold the edges of the dough over the filling, dampen them and roll up from the narrow edge, sealing well. Place seamside down into a well greased baking dish. Brush the roll all over with milk and scatter the remaining sugar on top. Bake in the oven for about 30 minutes, cover loosely with foil and continue baking until well browned. Spoon syrup sauce over the roll before serving with clotted cream or custard.

Oven	Conventional	Fan
Temperature	180°C	160°C
Preheating	Recommended	Not necessary
Shelf position	1st	1st
Time	1 hour	50 minutes

SYRUP SAUCE

60-75ml (4-5 tbsp) golden syrup
45ml (3 tbsp) water
30ml (2 tbsp) lemon juice

Warm the syrup and water gently in a saucepan, stir well then simmer for 2-3 minutes. Add lemon juice and serve warm over the Golden Syrup Roll.

COCONUT JAM PUDDING

Serves 4

50g (2oz) desiccated coconut
60ml (4 level tbsp) blackcurrant or plum jam
125g (4oz) butter or block margarine
finely grated rind of 1 lemon
125g (4oz) caster sugar
2 eggs, beaten · 125g (4oz) self raising flour
milk · sweet white sauce, to serve

Place a steamer over a pan two-thirds filled with water and bring to simmering point. Toast the coconut under a medium grill until golden brown. Cool. Lightly grease a 1.1 litre (2 pint) pudding basin and spoon the jam into the base. Beat the butter until soft, add the lemon rind and caster sugar, then cream together thoroughly. Beat in the eggs a little at a time and lastly fold in the flour and coconut. Add enough milk to give a fairly soft consistency. Spoon into the pudding basin, cover with greased greaseproof paper and foil and tie on securely. Steam for about 1¾ hours until just firm when pressed in the centre. Turn out on to a warmed plate and serve with a sweet white sauce.

BAKED ALASKA

Serves 6

225g (8oz) fresh or frozen raspberries
30ml (2 tbsp) orange-flavoured liqueur
one 20cm (8 inch) baked sponge flan
4 egg whites, at room temperature
175g (6oz) caster sugar
485ml (¾ pint) block vanilla ice cream

Place the fresh or frozen raspberries on a shallow dish and sprinkle over the liqueur. Cover and leave to marinate for 2 hours, turning occasionally. Place the sponge flan on a large ovenproof serving dish and spoon the raspberries with all their juices into the centre of the flan. Place the egg whites in a dry bowl and beat until the mixture stands in stiff peaks. Add 60ml (4 level tbsp) of the sugar and whisk, then spoon over the remaining sugar and fold through gently until no traces remain. Fit a good sized piping bag with a large star vegetable nozzle and spoon in the meringue mixture. Place the block of ice cream on top of the raspberries. Pipe the meringue on top, starting from the sponge base then around and over the ice cream until completely covered. Immediately place the completed Alaska in the oven for about 3 minutes. At this stage the meringue should be nicely tinged with brown. Watch the meringue carefully as it burns easily. Do not overcook or the ice cream will become too soft. Serve at once.

Oven	Conventional	Fan
Temperature	230°C	210°C
Preheating	Recommended	Recommended
Shelf position	2nd	2nd
Time	3-4 minutes	2-3 minutes

Baked Alaska

Top: Gooseberry Flan Bottom: Olde English Apple Pie

GOOSEBERRY FLAN

Serves 6

Pastry

200g (7oz) plain flour
pinch of salt
15g (½oz) caster sugar
125g (4oz) butter or block margarine
30ml (2 tbsp) cold water

Filling

700g (1½lb) gooseberries, fresh or frozen
75g (3oz) granulated sugar
150ml (¼ pint) water
15ml (1 level tbsp) arrowroot

Place a 20.5cm (8 inch) fluted or plain flan ring on an oven baking tray. For the pastry, sift together the flour, salt and sugar into a bowl. Rub in the butter or margarine until the mixture resembles fine breadcrumbs. Bind to a firm dough with the water. Roll out and line the flan ring. Lightly prick the pastry base. Cover with greased greaseproof paper and fill with baking beans. Bake 'blind' in the oven for 15 minutes. Remove the paper and beans, continue baking until the base is browned. Meanwhile, top and tail the gooseberries. Put the sugar and water into a pan, heat gently until the sugar is dissolved, then boil for 1-2 minutes. Put gooseberries into the syrup and cook gently for about 5 minutes until the gooseberries are just soft but still whole. Strain the liquid into a measuring jug and make up to 300ml (½ pint) if necessary with water. Blend the arrowroot in a bowl with some of the syrup, boil the remaining syrup, stir into the arrowroot mixture, return to the pan and stir over heat until boiled and thickened. Arrange drained gooseberries in the baked pastry case and cover them with the syrup. Serve warm or cold with pouring or whipped cream.

Oven	Conventional	Fan
Temperature	200°C	180°C
Preheating	Recommended	Recommended
Shelf position	1st	1st
Time	20-25 minutes	15-20 minutes

OLDE ENGLISH APPLE PIE

Serves 6

Pastry

225g (8oz) plain flour
pinch of salt
caster sugar
125g (4oz) butter or block margarine
45ml (3 tbsp) water

Filling

700g (1½lb) cooking apples, peeled, cored and sliced
125g (4oz) soft, light brown sugar
2.5ml (½ level tsp) ground cinnamon
1.25ml (¼ level tsp) ground nutmeg
finely grated rind and juice of ½ lemon
milk

For the pastry, sift the flour and salt into a mixing bowl, stir in 10ml (2 level tsp) caster sugar. Rub in the fat until the mixture resembles fine breadcrumbs. Stir in enough water to make a firm dough. Wrap in cling film and chill in the refrigerator for about 30 minutes. On a lightly floured working surface, roll out a little more than half the dough and use to line a 23cm (9 inch) pie plate. Put the apple slices into a bowl and stir in the brown sugar, cinnamon, nutmeg, lemon rind and juice. Spoon into the pie dish. Roll out the remaining pastry and use to cover the pie. Decorate with pastry leaves. Seal the edges well and make a slit in the centre for the steam to escape. Brush the top with milk and sprinkle a little caster sugar over. Bake in the oven at the higher temperature for 15 minutes then complete the cooking time at the lower temperature. Serve hot or cold with lightly whipped cream or custard.

Oven	Conventional	Fan
Temperature	200°C reduce to 180°C	180°C reduce to 160°C
Preheating	Recommended	Recommended
Shelf position	1st	1st
Time	45 minutes	35-40 minutes

PUDDINGS

PROFITEROLES WITH CHOCOLATE OR COFFEE CREAM SAUCE

Serves 4-6

Choux paste

| 150ml (¼ pint) water |
| 50g (2oz) butter |
| 65g (2½oz) plain flour, sifted |
| 2 eggs, beaten |

Put the water and butter into a saucepan, heat until the butter melts then bring to the boil. Remove the pan from the heat and quickly tip in the flour all at once. Beat well until the paste is smooth and forms a ball in the centre of the pan. Allow to cool for a minute or two. Beat in the eggs, a little at a time, beating vigorously to trap as much air as possible. Continue beating until the mixture is glossy. Fill the paste into a piping bag fitted with a 1cm (½ inch) plain vegetable nozzle. Wet two baking trays and pipe small balls of paste the size of a walnut 2.5cm (1 inch) apart. Bake in the oven for about 25 minutes until brown and crisp. Make a small slit in each one and return to the oven for 5 minutes to dry out the insides. Cool on a wire rack. Fill the profiteroles with 150ml (¼ pint) whipped double cream or Patisserie Cream. Pile into a serving dish.

Oven	Conventional	Fan
Temperature	220°C	200°C
Preheating	Recommended	Recommended
Shelf position	1st	1st
Time	25-30 minutes	20-25 minutes

CHOCOLATE SAUCE

| 225g (8oz) plain chocolate |
| 25g (1oz) butter |
| 90ml (6 tbsp) milk |
| 10ml (2 tsp) vanilla flavouring |

Break the chocolate into a basin placed over a pan of simmering water and allow the chocolate to melt. Beat the butter, milk and vanilla into the chocolate. Leave until cold then pour over the filled profiteroles.

COFFEE CREAM SAUCE

| 300ml (½ pint) double or whipping cream |
| 20-30ml (1½-2 tbsp) coffee essence |
| 10ml (2 level tsp) icing sugar, sifted |
| 25g (1oz) walnuts, finely chopped |

Whip the cream lightly until pouring consistency. Mix in the coffee essence, sugar and walnuts. Pour the sauce over the filled profiteroles.

PATISSERIE CREAM

| one egg |
| one egg yolk |
| 50g (2oz) caster sugar |
| 30ml (2 level tbsp) plain flour |
| 30ml (2 level tbsp) cornflour |
| 300ml (½ pint) milk |
| 1.25ml (¼ tsp) vanilla flavouring |

Put the whole egg, egg yolk and sugar into a bowl. Whisk together until smooth, then whisk in the flour, cornflour and a little of the milk. Heat the remaining milk almost to boiling, gradually whisk into the egg mixture. Pour into the pan and stir continuously over moderate heat for 1-2 minutes, whisking if necessary to keep it smooth, until thickened and cooked. Beat in the vanilla. Turn the mixture into a bowl, press cling film on top to prevent a skin forming and leave until cold. To fill the profiteroles, put patisserie cream into a piping bag fitted with a 5mm (¼ inch) plain nozzle and pipe into each choux. Pile them in a serving dish. Pour some chocolate or coffee cream sauce over and serve the remainder separately.

PUDDINGS

QUEEN OF PUDDINGS

Serves 4

400ml (¾ pint) milk
25g (1oz) butter
grated rind of 1 lemon
2 eggs, separated · 75g (3oz) caster sugar
75g (3oz) fresh white breadcrumbs
45ml (3 tbsp) raspberry jam

Warm the milk with the butter and lemon rind. Lightly whisk the egg yolks with 25g (1oz) of the sugar. Pour on the milk, stirring well. Strain the milk mixture over the breadcrumbs. Spread jam over the base of a greased 1.1 litre (2 pint) ovenproof dish. Pour crumb mixture into it. Bake in the oven for 25 minutes, until just set in the centre. Whisk the egg whites until stiff, whisk in half the remaining sugar, then gently fold in the rest. Pile the meringue on top of the pudding and bake for the remaining time, or until the meringue is lightly browned. Equally delicious served hot or cold.

Oven	Conventional	Fan
Temperature	180°C	160°C
Preheating	Recommended	Not necessary
Shelf position	1st	1st
Time	40 minutes	30-35 minutes

CARAMEL CUSTARD

Serves 4

140g (4½oz) caster sugar
150ml (¼ pint) water · 600ml (1 pint) milk
4 eggs, lightly beaten

Put 125g (4oz) of the sugar and the water into a small pan and dissolve the sugar over a gentle heat. When completely dissolved, bring to the boil without stirring until caramelised. Pour the caramel carefully into a 15cm (6 inch) round cake tin, turning the tin until the bottom is completely covered. Warm the milk, pour on to the eggs, add the remaining sugar and stir well. Strain over the cooled caramel. Place in a roasting tin (bain marie) and pour in sufficient hot water to come halfway up the side of the cake tin. Cover with foil and bake in the oven for about 50 minutes, or until set. Leave in the tin until quite cold, preferably overnight, before turning out.

Oven	Conventional	Fan
Temperature	170°C	150°C
Preheating	Not necessary	Not necessary
Shelf position	1st	1st
Time	1 hour	50-55 minutes

EVE'S PUDDING

Serves 4

450g (1lb) cooking apples, peeled, cored and sliced
25g (1oz) demerara sugar
grated rind of 1 lemon
75g (3oz) butter or block margarine
75g (3oz) caster sugar
one egg, lightly beaten
150g (5oz) self raising flour, sifted
30ml (2 tbsp) milk

Grease a 900ml (1½ pint) ovenproof dish. Place the prepared apples in the dish and sprinkle with the demerara sugar and lemon rind. Cream the butter with the sugar in a bowl until light and fluffy. Gradually beat in the egg. Fold in the flour with enough milk to give a dropping consistency. Spoon over the apples. Bake in the oven for about 40 minutes, until the apples are tender and a skewer inserted into the centre of the pudding comes out clean. Serve hot with custard.

Oven	Conventional	Fan
Temperature	170°C	150°C
Preheating	Recommended	Recommended
Shelf position	1st	1st
Time	50 minutes	40 minutes

BAKED APPLES

Serves 4

4 medium cooking apples, cored
90ml (6 level tbsp) mincemeat
60ml (4 tbsp) water

Make a shallow cut through the skin around the middle of each apple. Stand them in an ovenproof dish and fill with the mincemeat. Pour the water around the apples. Bake in the oven for about 1 hour until the apples are soft when tested with a skewer. Serve hot.

Oven	Conventional	Fan
Temperature	190°C	170°C
Preheating	Not necessary	Not necessary
Shelf position	1st	1st
Time	1 hour	45 minutes

Top: Queen of Puddings Bottom: Caramel Custard

RHUBARB & GINGER CRUMBLE
Serves 4

700g (1½lb) rhubarb, trimmed
125g (4oz) demerara sugar
5ml (1 level tsp) ground ginger
finely grated rind and juice of 1 orange

Crumble

225g (8oz) plain flour
125g (4oz) butter or block margarine
50g (2oz) soft brown sugar

Cut the rhubarb into 2.5cm (1 inch) lengths. Mix together the sugar, ginger and orange rind. Place the rhubarb in an ovenproof dish. Sprinkle with the sugar mixture and pour over the orange juice. For the crumble, sift the flour into a bowl and rub in the fat until the mixture resembles fine breadcrumbs. Stir in the sugar, then sprinkle the crumble over the rhubarb. Bake in the oven for about 35 minutes, until the rhubarb is tender and the crumble golden brown. Serve hot or cold with custard or whipped cream.

Oven	Conventional	Fan
Temperature	190°C	170°C
Preheating	Recommended	Not necessary
Shelf position	1st	1st
Time	35-40 minutes	30-35 minutes

EGG CUSTARD TART
Serves 4-6

shortcrust pastry, made with 175g (6oz) plain flour
2 eggs · 30ml (2 level tbsp) caster sugar
300ml (½ pint) milk · ground nutmeg

Roll out the dough and use to line an 18cm (7 inch) flan ring. Cover the base with foil and fill with baking beans. Bake 'blind' in the oven at the higher temperature until lightly browned and the base dry, removing the foil and beans during the final 5 minutes. Put the eggs and sugar into a bowl and whisk together. Warm the milk and lightly whisk into the egg mixture. Strain the custard into the pastry case and sprinkle the top with nutmeg. Bake in the oven at the lower temperature for about 25 minutes, or until the filling is set and lightly browned. Serve cold.

Oven	Conventional	Fan
Temperature	200°C reduce to 180°C	180°C reduce to 160°C
Preheating	Recommended	Recommended
Shelf position	1st	1st
Time	Pastry 20-25 minutes Filling 25-30 minutes	15-20 minutes 20-25 minutes

GERMAN CHEESECAKE WITH MERINGUE TOPPING
Serves 8

Pastry

225g (8oz) plain flour
1.25ml (¼ level tsp) salt
125g (4oz) butter or block margarine
50g (2oz) caster sugar
30-45ml (2-3 tbsp) cold water

Filling

225g (8oz) cottage cheese
4 egg yolks
125g (4oz) caster sugar
25g (1oz) ground almonds
finely grated rind of 1 lemon
one 142ml (5floz) carton soured cream
50g (2oz) sultanas
50g (2oz) mixed peel, finely chopped

Meringue

2 egg whites
125g (4oz) caster sugar

For the pastry, sift the flour and salt into a bowl. Rub in the fat until the mixture resembles fine breadcrumbs. Mix in the sugar. Add enough cold water to bind to a fairly firm dough. Roll out the dough and use to line a tin measuring about 18cm x 28cm (7 x 11 inch). Pinch the edges to decorate. Cover the base with foil and fill with baking beans. Bake 'blind' in the oven at the higher temperature for about 15 minutes. Remove the foil and beans, continue cooking for 7-10 minutes until the pastry is cooked. For the filling, process or sieve the cottage cheese until smooth. Put the egg yolks and sugar into a bowl, beat until pale and creamy. Mix in the ground almonds, lemon rind, soured cream, sultanas, peel and cottage cheese. Spread the mixture in the pastry case. For the meringue, whisk the egg whites until stiff. Whisk in half the sugar, then stir in the remainder. Using a piping bag and a 5mm (¼ inch) plain nozzle, pipe the meringue in straight lines across the tin over the filling. Bake in the oven at the lower temperature for about 1 hour, until the meringue is lightly browned and crisp and the filling is set. Switch off the oven and leave the cheesecake in until cooled.

Oven	Conventional	Fan
Temperature	200°C reduce to 140°C	180°C reduce to 120°C
Preheating	Recommended	Recommended
Shelf position	1st	1st
Time	1 hour 50 minutes	1½ hours

PUDDINGS

CHOCOLATE SURPRISE PUDDING

Serves 4

| 125g (4oz) self raising flour |
| 30ml (2 level tbsp) cocoa powder |
| pinch of salt |
| 150g (5oz) caster sugar |
| 150ml (¼ pint) milk |
| 30ml (2 tbsp) vegetable oil |
| 5ml (1 tsp) vanilla flavouring |
| 50g (2oz) walnuts, roughly chopped |
| 125g (4oz) soft, light brown sugar |
| 300ml (½ pint) boiling water |

Grease a 1.1 litre (2 pint) ovenproof dish. Sift together the flour, 15ml (1 level tbsp) of the cocoa and the salt. Stir in the caster sugar. Make a well in the centre and pour in the milk, oil and vanilla. Whisk together until smooth and creamy. Stir in the walnuts. Pour the mixture into the dish. Mix the remaining cocoa and the brown sugar together and sprinkle over the pudding mixture. Gently pour the boiling water evenly over the surface of the pudding. Bake in the oven for about 45 minutes, until well risen. During baking, the sauce will sink to the bottom of the dish and the sponge will rise on top. Serve hot.

Oven	Conventional	Fan
Temperature	180°C	160°C
Preheating	Recommended	Not necessary
Shelf position	1st	1st
Time	50 minutes	45 minutes

CREME BRULEE

Serves 6

| 300ml (½ pint) double cream |
| 300ml (½ pint) single cream |
| 4 egg yolks |
| 75g (3oz) caster sugar |
| 5ml (1 tsp) vanilla flavouring |

Put all the cream into a saucepan and warm gently on low hob heat but do not boil. Meanwhile put the egg yolks, 25g (1oz) of the caster sugar and the vanilla in a mixing bowl and beat thoroughly. Pour the heated cream on to the egg mixture and mix well. Pour into 6 individual ramekin dishes and place in a roasting tin (bain marie) and pour in sufficient hot water to come halfway up the sides of the dishes. Bake in the oven for about 35 minutes, or until just set. Remove from the roasting tin and allow to cool, then chill in the refrigerator for several hours, preferably overnight. Heat the grill. Sprinkle the top of each custard with the remaining sugar to completely cover. Put dishes under the preheated hot grill until the sugar begins to caramelise. Serve immediately.

Oven	Conventional	Fan
Temperature	150°C	130°C
Preheating	Not necessary	Not necessary
Shelf position	1st	1st
Time	45 minutes	35-40 minutes

PAVLOVA

Serves 6-8

| 3 egg whites |
| 175g (6oz) caster sugar |
| 5ml (1 level tsp) cornflour |
| 5ml (1 tsp) vinegar |
| 2.5ml (½ tsp) vanilla flavouring |
| 300ml (½ pint) double cream |
| 225g (8oz) strawberries, hulled |

Draw a 23cm (9 inch) circle on non-stick paper and place on a baking sheet. Whisk the egg whites until stiff but not dry. Gradually whisk in half the sugar, then gently fold in the remainder together with the cornflour, vinegar and vanilla. Spread two-thirds of the meringue mixture over the circle, spoon the remainder around the outside edge to form a wall. Bake in the oven for about 1 hour, until the meringue is crisp on the outside and slightly soft inside. Leave until cold. Carefully remove the paper and place the meringue on a serving plate. Whip the cream until thick and pile into the shell with some of the strawberries. Place the remaining strawberries on top to decorate.

Oven	Conventional	Fan
Temperature	130°C	110°C
Preheating	Not necessary	Not necessary
Shelf position	1st	1st
Time	1¼ hours	1 hour

PUDDINGS

LEMON MERINGUE PIE
Serves 4-6

shortcrust pastry, made with 175g (6oz) plain flour
45ml (3 level tbsp) cornflour
150ml (¼ pint) water
grated rind and juice of 2 lemons
125g (4oz) sugar
2 eggs, separated
75g (3oz) caster sugar

Roll out the dough and use to line an 18cm (7 inch) flan ring. Cover the base with foil and fill with baking beans. Bake 'blind' in the oven at the higher temperature until lightly browned and the base dry, removing the foil and beans during the final 5 minutes. Mix the cornflour with the water in a saucepan. Add the lemon rind and juice and bring slowly to the boil, stirring until the mixture thickens. Add the 125g (4oz) sugar. Remove from the heat, cool the mixture slightly and beat in the egg yolks, one at a time. Pour into the pastry case. Whisk the egg whites stiffly, whisk in half the caster sugar and then fold in the remainder. Pile the meringue on top of the lemon filling. Bake in the oven at the lower temperature until the meringue is crisp and lightly browned. Serve warm or cold.

Oven	Conventional	Fan
Temperature	200°C reduce to 180°C	180°C reduce to 160°C
Preheating	Recommended	Recommended
Shelf position	1st	1st
Time	Pastry 20-25 minutes Meringue 15-20 minutes	15-20 minutes 10-15 minutes

MILLE-FEUILLES SLICE
Serves 6

one 212g (7½oz) packet frozen puff pastry
200ml (⅓ pint) double cream
30ml (2 tbsp) raspberry jam
60ml (4 tbsp) white glâcé icing
pink food colouring
25g (1oz) chopped nuts

Roll out the pastry very thinly to a rectangle measuring 25.5 x 38cm (10 x 15 inch). Trim the edges and cut into three smaller rectangles measuring 25.5 x 12.5cm (10 x 5 inch). Place on a wetted baking sheet, prick well, and bake in the oven for about 8 minutes, until well risen, crisp and golden brown. Cool on a wire rack. Meanwhile, whisk the cream until it just holds its shape.

Sandwich the pastry slices together with the jam and the cream. Colour the icing pink and spread over the slice. Decorate the edges with the chopped nuts.

Oven	Conventional	Fan
Temperature	230°C	210°C
Preheating	Recommended	Recommended
Shelf position	1st	1st
Time	10 minutes	8 minutes

CHOCOLATE ROULADE
Serves 6-8

4 large eggs, separated
175g (6oz) caster sugar
40g (1½oz) cocoa powder
icing sugar, to dredge
300ml (½ pint) double cream

Brush a 20 x 30 x 2.5cm (8 x 12 x 1 inch) Swiss roll tin with oil and line with non-stick paper, cutting diagonally into the corners to give a neat lining. Place the egg whites into a large bowl and the yolks into another. Whisk the whites until stiff but not dry. Add the sugar to the yolks and whisk together until thick and smooth. Sift the cocoa powder into the yolk mixture, stir quickly and evenly then fold in the egg white gently but thoroughly. Spread the mixture in the prepared tin. Bake in the oven for about 20 minutes or until the mixture feels springy all over when lightly pressed. Meanwhile, sift some icing sugar over a large piece of greaseproof paper, and thoroughly wring out a tea towel which has been soaked in hot water. Immediately the roulade is cooked, turn it on to the sugared paper. Carefully remove the lining paper and cover the roulade with the damp tea towel to retain the moisture. Leave for at least 1 hour to become cold and set. With a sharp knife, trim off all the crusty sides. Whip the cream until thick and spread over the roulade. Holding the narrow end, roll up away from you to the opposite narrow end. Put join side down on to a serving plate and dredge generously with sifted icing sugar.

Oven	Conventional	Fan
Temperature	180°C	160°C
Preheating	Recommended	Recommended
Shelf position	1st	1st
Time	20-25 minutes	18-20 minutes

Top: Lemon Meringue Pie Bottom: Mille-Feuilles Slice

Batch Cooking

PIZZAS

All the recipes on this page are for one oven load. They should be prepared as suggested and baked at the same time at the shelf positions recommended.

FAN OVEN BATCH COOKING

These pizzas and the following recipes demonstrate how quantities of food can be cooked in the fan oven all at once. A distinct advantage when packing the freezer and when entertaining.

PIZZA BASE

For each of three trays

450g (1lb) packet bread mix, white or brown
liquid as directed on the packet

Make up the mix as directed on the packet. Roll out to a rectangle the size of an oven baking tray to within 5cm (2 inch) of the edges. Grease the tray, place the dough on it. Cover with cling film and leave in a warm place for about 30 minutes to prove. Three packets of bread mix can be made together to cover three baking trays and allowed to prove while making the toppings.

TRADITIONAL PIZZA

Tray 1. To cover one bread dough base

30ml (2 tbsp) vegetable oil
175g (6oz) onion, chopped
2 garlic cloves, skinned and crushed
one 800g (1lb 12oz) can tomatoes
5ml (1 level tsp) dried basil
5ml (1 level tsp) dried oregano
225g (8oz) mushrooms, wiped and sliced
2 bay leaves
salt and pepper
175g (6oz) sliced Mozarella cheese

Heat the oil in a large frying pan and fry the onion for about 5 minutes until lightly browned. Stir in the garlic, tomatoes, basil, oregano, mushrooms, bay leaves and seasoning. Cook until the mixture is thick and pulpy. Remove the bay leaves and spread mixture evenly over the proved bread dough. Arrange the Mozarella cheese on top. Bake in the oven on the 1st shelf for about 20 minutes, until the cheese melts and browns slightly.

PRAWN AND CREAM CHEESE PIZZA

Tray 2. To cover one bread dough base

375g (12oz) cream cheese
90ml (6 tbsp) double cream
225g (8oz) prawns
4 spring onions, trimmed and chopped
10ml (2 level tsp) dried dill
salt and pepper
50g (2oz) grated Parmesan cheese

Mix together the cream cheese and cream. Stir in the prawns, onion, dill and seasoning. Spread the mixture evenly over the proved bread dough. Cover with cheese. Bake in the oven on the 2nd shelf for about 20 minutes, until the cheese is lightly browned.

VEGETABLE PIZZA

Tray 3. To cover one bread dough base

60ml (4 tbsp) vegetable oil
175g (6oz) onions, sliced
225g (8oz) courgettes, thinly sliced
225g (8oz) aubergines, cut in matchsticks
225g (8oz) tomatoes, sliced
30ml (2 level tbsp) tomato purée
salt and pepper
75g (3oz) thinly sliced Cheddar cheese
75g (3oz) thinly sliced Red Leicester cheese

Heat the oil in a large frying pan and fry the onion for about 5 minutes until lightly coloured. Mix in the courgettes, aubergines, tomatoes, purée and seasoning. Cook for about 5 minutes until the vegetables are softening. Spread the mixture evenly over the proved bread dough. Arrange the Cheddar cheese and Red Leicester cheese slices in joining rows across the mixture. Bake in the oven on the 4th shelf for about 20 minutes, until the cheese melts and browns slightly.

Fan oven or intensive bake*	
Temperature	200°C
Preheating	Not necessary
Shelf position	1st, 2nd, 4th
Time	About 20 minutes

*If baking just one pizza intensive bake may be used. Shelf position 1 or 2.

QUICHES

QUICHES

For four quiches

Pastry	900g (2lb) plain flour
	10ml (2 level tsp) salt
	350g (12oz) block margarine · 225g (8oz) lard
	150ml (¼ pint) cold water

Sift together the flour and salt into a bowl. Rub in the margarine and lard until the mixture resembles breadcrumbs. Mix in enough water to give a fairly firm dough. Roll out the pastry in portions and line; two 25.5cm (10 inch) quiche dishes, two 28 x 18cm (11 x 7 inch) shallow baking tins. Prick the bases lightly, cover with greaseproof paper and fill with baking beans. Bake 'blind' in the oven at the higher temperature for 20-25 minutes. Remove the paper and beans, during the final 5 minutes cooking time.

ONION AND CHEESE

Serves 6-8. Use a quiche dish

50g (2oz) butter or margarine
450(1lb) onions, thinly sliced
15ml (1 tbsp) vinegar · salt and pepper
60ml (4 tbsp) chopped fresh parsley
3 eggs · 15ml (1 level tbsp) plain flour
150ml (¼ pint) single cream · 75ml (2½floz) milk
125g (4oz) grated mature Cheddar cheese

Melt the butter or margarine in a frying pan and gently cook the onions for 10-15 minutes until softened and lightly browned. Stir in the vinegar, parsley and seasoning. Leave to cool, then spread the onions in the baked pastry case. Whisk together the eggs, flour, cream and milk. Stir in the cheese and pour the mixture over the onions. Bake in the oven on the 1st or 4th shelf at the lower temperature for 35-40 minutes, until just set in the centre.

BROCCOLI AND CHEESE

Serves 6-8. Use a rectangular tin

225g (8oz) cooked broccoli, well drained and roughly chopped
175g (6oz) crumbled Lancashire cheese
2 eggs · salt and pepper
150ml (¼ pint) single cream

Spread the broccoli in the baked pastry case and cover with the cheese. Whisk the eggs with cream and seasoning. Pour the mixture over the cheese. Bake in the oven on the 2nd shelf at the lower temperature for 35-40 minutes, until just set in the centre.

Left: Quiches and Cream of Lemon Soup (see page 59 for recipe).

ASPARAGUS, HAM AND CHEESE

Serves 6-8. Use a rectangular tin

one 340g (12oz) can asparagus, well drained
125g (4oz) cooked ham, diced
3 eggs
225g (8oz) cream cheese
10ml (2 level tsp) French mustard
300ml (½ pint) milk
salt and pepper

Arrange the asparagus in the baked pastry case and add the ham. Whisk the eggs with the cream cheese, mustard, milk and seasoning. Pour the mixture over the asparagus. Bake in the oven on the 2nd shelf at the lower temperature for 35-40 minutes, until just set in the centre.

MUSHROOM, PEPPER AND CHEESE

Serves 6-8. Use a quiche dish

50g (2oz) butter or margarine
one small green pepper, deseeded and finely chopped
one small red pepper, deseeded and finely chopped
6 spring onions, trimmed and chopped
450g (1lb) button mushrooms, wiped & thinly sliced
40g (1½oz) plain flour
300ml (½ pint) milk, heated with 1 bay leaf, parsley sprigs and a piece of onion, strained
one egg, beaten
salt and pepper
125g (4oz) grated Gruyère or Cheddar cheese

Melt the butter or margarine in a saucepan and cook the peppers for about 10 minutes until softened. Mix in the onions and mushrooms and cook for 2-3 minutes until softened. Whisk together the flour, milk, egg and seasoning. Add to the pan and cook for 1-2 minutes, stirring. Mix in most of the cheese. Pour the mixture into the baked pastry case, sprinkle remaining cheese on top. Bake in the oven on the 1st or 4th shelf at the lower temperature for 35-40 minutes, until just set in the centre.

Fan oven only	
Temperature	Pastry 180°C Quiche 160°C
Preheating	Recommended
Shelf position	1st, 2nd, 4th
Time	Pastry 20-25 minutes Quiche 35-40 minutes

FINGER FOOD

SPICED CHICKEN DRUMSTICKS
Tray 3.

8 chicken drumsticks, skinned and pierced all over with a knife	
Baste	30ml (2 level tbsp) honey
	15ml (1 tbsp) soy sauce
	30ml (2 tbsp) lemon juice
	30ml (2 level tbsp) tomato ketchup
	5ml (1 level tsp) dried tarragon · pepper

Butter a piece of foil, fold up the edges all round and place on half a baking tray. Put the honey, soy sauce, lemon juice, tomato ketchup, tarragon and pepper into a saucepan. Stir over heat until blended. Arrange the drumsticks on the foil and spoon half the baste over them. Bake in the oven on 4th shelf for 15 minutes, turn the drumsticks over, spoon the remaining baste over them and continue baking for 15-20 minutes, until tender.

CRISPY POTATO CHEESE ROUNDS
Tray 1. Makes 34

700g (1½lb) potatoes, boiled and mashed	
2 egg yolks	
50g (2oz) finely grated mature Cheddar cheese	
25g (1oz) grated Parmesan cheese	
5ml (1 level tsp) English mustard	
salt and pepper	
Coating	50g (2oz) medium oatmeal
	125g (4oz) salted peanuts, chopped
	one egg, beaten with 10ml (2 tsp) water

Butter the oven baking tray. Mix the potatoes with the egg yolks, Cheddar and Parmesan cheese, mustard and seasoning. Shape into balls. Mix together the oatmeal and peanuts. Coat the potato rounds with beaten egg, then with the oatmeal and peanuts mixture. Arrange the potato rounds on the tray. Bake in the oven on the 1st or 2nd shelf for about 20 minutes, until lightly browned. Serve on cocktail sticks.

SAUSAGES ON STICKS
Tray 2.

450g (1lb) cocktail sausages
oil, to brush

Brush half an oven baking tray with oil. Add the sausages and brush them with oil. Bake in the oven for about 20 minutes until brown, turning them at least once. Serve on cocktail sticks.

KIDNEY BACON ROLLS
Tray 2. Makes 32

8 lamb's kidneys, trimmed and quartered
16 streaky bacon rashers, about 450g (1lb), rinded

Place a piece of foil folded well up round the edges on half an oven baking tray with the sausages. Cut the rashers in half and stretch them thinly with the back of a knife. Roll the bacon round each kidney quarter and secure with halved cocktail sticks. Arrange join side down on the foil. Bake in the oven on the 1st or 2nd shelf for about 20 minutes, until the bacon is crisp.

SAVOURY MEAT BALLS
Tray 3. Makes about 24 balls

450g (1lb) minced beef
½ small red pepper, deseeded
½ small green pepper, deseeded
125g (4oz) onion · 25g (1oz) bread
10ml (2 tsp) Worcestershire sauce
one size 1 or 2 (large) egg, beaten
salt and pepper
oil, to brush

Brush oil over half a baking tray. Process or mince the beef with the red and green peppers, onion and bread. Mix in the Worcestershire sauce, egg and seasoning. Shape the mixture into 2.5cm (1 inch) size balls. Arrange them on the tray and brush with oil. Bake in the oven on the 4th shelf for about 15 minutes, turn the balls over, brush with oil and continue baking for another 15 minutes, until tender. Serve hot on sticks with Spicy Tomato Dip.

SPICY TOMATO DIP

25g (1oz) margarine
one medium onion, finely chopped
450(1lb) tomatoes, skinned and chopped
30ml (2 level tbsp) chilli seasoning
salt and pepper

Melt the margarine in a pan and gently fry the onion for 2-3 minutes. Mix in the tomatoes, chilli seasoning and seasoning. Cook for about 20 minutes until the mixture is thick. Serve hot or cold.

Fan oven only	
Temperature	170°C
Preheating	Not necessary
Shelf position	1st, 2nd, 4th
Time	20-30 minutes

AL FRESCO FOOD

All the recipes on this page are for one oven load. They should be prepared as suggested and baked at the same time at the shelf positions recommended

STUFFED COURGETTES
Tray 1

2-3 large courgettes · 25g (1oz) butter
125g (4oz) onion, finely chopped
2-3 tomatoes, skinned and chopped
1.25ml (¼ level tsp) dried basil
40g (1½oz) fresh breadcrumbs
25g (1oz) nuts, finely chopped
25g (1oz) grated cheese · salt and pepper

Use half an oven baking tray with the sweetcorn. Butter a piece of foil, place on half of the tray, folding up the edges all round. Cut the courgettes in half lengthways. Scoop out the seeds to leave the centres hollow. Melt the butter in a pan and fry the onion until softened and golden brown. Mix in the tomatoes, basil, breadcrumbs and nuts. Remove the pan from the heat, mix in the cheese and seasoning. Press the mixture into the hollow of each courgette and arrange on the foil. Bake in the oven on the 1st or 2nd shelf for about 15 minutes, until courgettes are just tender when pierced with a skewer.

STUFFED MUSHROOMS
Tray 1

8 large flat mushrooms, wiped and stalks removed
25g (1oz) butter
50g (2oz) bacon rashers, rinded and finely chopped
small bunch spring onions, include green ends, trimmed and finely chopped
50g (2oz) fresh breadcrumbs
10ml (2 tsp) lemon juice
2.5ml (¼ level tsp) dried thyme
30ml (2 tbsp) milk · salt and pepper

Use half an oven baking tray with the tomatoes. Butter the tray and add the mushrooms. Chop the mushroom stalks. Melt butter in a pan and fry the bacon, onions, and mushroom stalks until softened. Remove from the heat and stir in the breadcrumbs, lemon juice, thyme, milk and seasoning. Divide and press the mixture on to each mushroom. Bake in the oven on the 1st or 2nd shelf for about 15 minutes, until the stuffing is lightly browned.

Fan Oven only	
Temperature	180°C
Preheating	Not necessary
Shelf position	1st, 2nd, 4th
Time	15 minutes And 1 hour for potatoes and onions

STUFFED TOMATOES
Tray 2

8 medium tomatoes · 30ml (2 tbsp) vegetable oil
one garlic clove, skinned and crushed
one medium onion, finely chopped
one 425g (15oz) can chick peas, drained
45ml (3 tbsp) chopped fresh parsley
salt and pepper

Use half an oven baking tray with the mushrooms. Cut a slice from the base of each tomato (opposite end to the stalks), reserve. Scoop out the seeds and stand the tomatoes upside down to drain. Heat the oil in a pan and fry the garlic and onion until softened. Mash the chick peas a little, stir into the pan with the parsley and seasoning. Fill the tomatoes with the mixture. Place the tomato slices on top and arrange on the tray. Bake in the oven on the 1st or 2nd shelf for about 15 minutes, until the tomatoes are just tender.

LEMON SWEETCORN
Tray 2

2 corn on the cob, each cut in 3 portions
25g (1oz) butter, softened
finely grated rind of one lemon · salt and pepper

Use half the oven baking tray with the courgettes, place a piece of foil on the tray folding up the edges all round. Arrange the sweetcorn on the foil. Mix together the butter, lemon rind and seasoning. Spread the flavoured butter over the sweetcorn. Bake in the oven on the 1st or 2nd shelf for about 15 minutes, until the corn is tender.

BAKED ONIONS & POTATOES
Tray 3

eight 125-175g (4-6oz) potatoes, scrubbed
eight 125-175g (4-6oz) onions, skinned
40g (1½oz) butter, softened
7.5ml (1½ level tsp) caster sugar
7.5ml (1½ tsp) vinegar · salt and pepper

Place a piece of foil folded up all round the edges on half the oven baking tray with the potatoes. Put the onions into a saucepan with water to cover. Bring to the boil and simmer for 10 minutes, then drain well. Scoop out some onion from the top centre of each and place the onions on the foil. Mix together the butter, sugar, vinegar and seasoning and place some of the mixture in the top of each onion. Bake in the oven on the 4th shelf for up to 1 hour, until tender when pierced at the base with a skewer. Place 8 scrubbed, pricked jacket potatoes alongside onions, bake until tender when squeezed.

SHORTBREAD & MERINGUES

SHORTBREAD BASE

Grease three oven baking trays

Shortbread base

225g (8oz) plain flour
25g (1oz) cornflour
175g (6oz) butter
75g (3oz) caster sugar

Sift the flour and cornflour into a bowl. Rub in the butter until the mixture resembles breadcrumbs. Mix in the sugar and knead lightly to a dough. Press the mixture thoroughly and evenly on to the baking tray to within 5cm (2 inches) of the edges. Prick all over with a fork.

Fan Oven only	
Temperature	160°C
Preheating	Not necessary
Shelf position	1st, 2nd, 4th
Time	20 minutes

SHORTBREAD STREUSEL

Tray 1

225g (8oz) raspberry jam
175g (6oz) plain flour
75g (3oz) butter
50g (2oz) caster sugar

Make up the shortbread base, press on to the oven baking tray and prick all over. Smooth the jam over the top. Put the flour into a bowl, rub in the butter and mix in the sugar. Lightly press the crumble over the jam. Bake in the oven on the 1st shelf for 20 minutes, until lightly browned. Cool for about 5 minutes, then cut into fingers or squares while still warm. Cool on a wire rack. When cold, store in an airtight container.

APRICOT WALNUT SHORTBREAD

Tray 2

125g (4oz) dried apricots, finely chopped
50g (2oz) walnuts, finely chopped

Make up the shortbread base and mix in the apricots and walnuts. Press the mixture on to the baking tray and prick all over. Bake in the oven on the 2nd shelf for 20 minutes, until lightly browned. Cool for about 5 minutes, then cut into squares or fingers while still warm. Cool on a wire rack. When cold, store in an airtight container.

Top: Shortbread   Bottom: Meringues

CHOCOLATE CARAMEL SHORTBREAD

Tray 3

half 397g (14oz) can condensed milk
225g (8oz) butter
225g (8oz) light soft brown sugar
60ml (4 level tbsp) golden syrup
2.5ml (½ tsp) vanilla flavouring
283g (10oz) grated plain chocolate

Make up the shortbread base, press on to the baking tray and prick all over. Bake in the oven on the 4th shelf for 20 minutes, until lightly browned. Leave to cool. Put the condensed milk, butter, sugar and syrup into a saucepan, stir over a gentle heat until the sugar is dissolved. Bring to the boil and cook for about 7 minutes, until a little of the mixture dropped into cold water forms a soft ball when squeezed with the fingers 103°C (217°F). Quickly spread the caramel mixture over the baked shortbread base. Scatter the grated chocolate over the warm caramel so that it melts without being spread. Leave until set and cut into fingers or squares with a large sharp knife. When cold, store in an airtight container.

MERINGUES

8 egg whites · 450g (1lb) caster sugar

Cover three baking trays with silicone (non-stick) paper. Make up the meringue in two or three batches. Put the egg whites into a grease-free bowl. Whisk in half the sugar, sprinkling in about 15ml (1 level tbsp) at a time. Lightly fold in the remaining sugar. Use a piping bag fitted with a large fluted pipe.

MERINGUE NESTS

Tray 1. Mark six to eight 5cm (2 inch) circles on the non-stick paper. Pipe the meringue to cover each circle and form the nest base. Pipe a border on the base around the edge to make a good hollow in the centre. Dry out in the oven for 2½-3 hours. Cool on a wire rack. When cold, fill the centres with Chocolate Mousse, top with whipped cream and decorate with chocolate flakes or crystallised violets.

MERINGUE TRANCHE

Tray 2. Mark two rectangles measuring about 25.5 x 13cm (10 x 5 inch). Pipe the meringue in joining lines across each rectangle to form two separate layers. Dry out in the oven for 2½-3 hours. Cool on a wire rack. When cold, place one layer on a serving dish. Cover with fresh or well drained fruits and whipped cream. Cover with the remaining meringue layer.

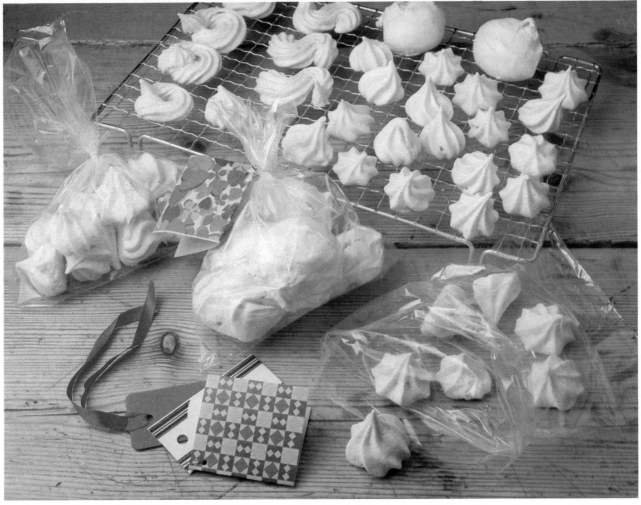

MERINGUES & SCONES

MERINGUE SWIRLS

Tray 3. Pipe the meringue into swirls about 2.5cm (1 inch) across the base. Dry out in the oven for 2½-3 hours. Cool on a wire rack. When cold, store in an airtight tin. Use swirls to decorate sides of gâteaux, arrange on top of trifles. Serve with other desserts or crumble into whipped cream to serve fresh or frozen.

Fan Oven only	
Temperature	160°C
Preheating	Recommended
Shelf position	1st, 2nd, 4th
Time	2½-3 hours

CHOCOLATE MOUSSE

175g (6oz) plain chocolate
3 egg yolks · 2 egg whites
15ml (1 tbsp) brandy or a few drops of vanilla flavouring
150ml (¼ pint) double cream, whipped

Melt the chocolate in a pan on low hob heat or in a bowl over a pan of hot water. Beat the egg yolks into the chocolate and add the brandy or vanilla. Whisk the egg whites until just stiff, fold lightly into the mousse. Chill to set.

CHEESE SCONES

Tray 1

450g (1lb) self raising flour
5ml (1 level tsp) salt
10ml (2 level tsp) baking powder
5ml (1 level tsp) mustard powder
125g (4oz) block margarine
125g (4oz) grated cheese
150ml (¼ pint) natural yoghurt made up to 225ml (8floz) with milk
milk and poppy seeds, to coat

Sift together the flour, salt, baking powder and mustard powder into a bowl. Rub in the margarine. Stir in the cheese, add the yoghurt mixture and bind to a fairly firm dough. Roll out and cut into 5cm (2 inch) plain rounds. Brush with milk and sprinkle with poppy seeds if liked. Place on an oven baking tray. Bake in the oven for 8-12 minutes until well risen and browned. Cool on wire racks.

FIG AND BROWN SUGARED SCONES

Tray 2

350g (12oz) self raising wholewheat flour
125g (4oz) white self raising flour
5ml (1 level tsp) salt
10ml (2 level tsp) baking powder
125g (4oz) block margarine
125g (4oz) dried figs, chopped
75g (3oz) soft brown sugar · 225ml (8floz) milk
25ml (1½ level tbsp) honey and 7g (¼oz) butter, to brush

Mix the flours, salt and baking powder into a bowl. Rub in the margarine. Mix in the figs and sugar. Add the milk and bind to a fairly firm dough. Roll out and cut into 5cm (2 inch) fluted rounds. Warm together the honey and butter, brush liberally over the scones. Place on an oven baking tray. Bake in the oven for 8-12 minutes, until well risen and browned. Cool on wire racks.

SPICED SULTANA AND ORANGE SCONES

Tray 3

450g (1lb) self raising flour · 5ml (1 level tsp) salt
10ml (2 level tsp) baking powder
125g (4oz) block margarine
grated rind of one large orange
75g (3oz) caster sugar
10ml (2 level tsp) ground cinnamon
125g (4oz) sultanas · 225ml (8floz) milk
15ml (1 tbsp) orange juice and 25ml (1½ level tbsp) golden syrup to brush

Sift together the flour, salt and baking powder into a bowl. Rub in the margarine. Mix in the orange rind, sugar cinnamon and sultanas. Add the milk and mix to a fairly firm dough. Roll out and cut into 5cm (2 inch) fluted rounds. Mix together the orange juice and syrup, brush liberally over the scones. Place on an oven baking tray. Bake in the oven for 8-12 minutes, until well risen and golden brown. Cool on wire racks.

Fan Oven only	
Temperature	200°C
Preheating	Recommended
Shelf position	1st, 2nd, 4th
Time	10-12 minutes

Note: All scones may be served warm or cold, split and spread with butter and preserves.

CAKES

VICTORIA SPONGE MIX

Makes: Coffee and Coconut Squares. Frosted Peppermint and Chocolate Fingers. Cream Meringue Gâteau. Chocolate Cakes, Cherry Almond Cakes. Jam or Cream Fancies.

1st Shelf

450g (1lb) butter or soft tub margarine
450g (1lb) caster sugar
8 eggs, beaten · 450g (1lb) self raising flour

Beat together the butter and sugar in a bowl until soft and fluffy. Gradually beat in the eggs, adding a little sifted flour with the last of the egg. Fold in the remaining sifted flour. Grease and base line two shallow rectangular tins, measuring about 18 x 28cm (7 x 11 inch). Grease and base line two 20.5cm (8 inch) round sandwich tins. Arrange twenty paper cake cases on an oven baking tray. Fit racks on to the 1st and 2nd shelves in the oven. Rectangular tins: Take about half of the prepared sponge mixture, put half into one bowl and half into another. Flavour each half separately.

COFFEE AND COCONUT SQUARES

Add 50g (2oz) desiccated coconut and 30ml (2 tbsp) coffee essence. Spread in a rectangular tin.

FROSTED PEPPERMINT AND CHOCOLATE FINGERS:

Halve the mixture adding peppermint essence and green food colouring to one half. Swirl together the plain and flavoured mixtures in a rectangular tin. Bake both tins in the oven on the 1st shelf for about 20-30 minutes, until just firm to the touch. Cool on a wire rack. **To finish:** Coffee and Coconut: Dredge generously with sifted icing sugar and cut into squares. Peppermint and Chocolate: Cover with chocolate frosting. When set, cut into fingers.

CHOCOLATE FROSTING

15ml (1 level tbsp) cocoa powder
15ml (1 tbsp) warm water
75g (3oz) butter, softened
225g (8oz) icing sugar, sifted

Mix together the cocoa powder and warm water in a saucepan until smooth. Add the butter and melt over a gentle heat. Tip in all the icing sugar, beat to mix evenly and swirl quickly over the cake.

Fan oven only	
Temperature	160°C
Preheating	Recommended
Shelf position	1st, 2nd, 4th
Time	See individual recipes

CREAM MERINGUE GATEAU

2nd Shelf

Round tins: Take about half of the remaining sponge mixture and spread in the tins. Bake in the oven on the 2nd shelf for about 17 minutes, until just firm to the touch. Cool on a wire rack. To finish: Spread one sponge with about 30ml (2 level tbsp) apricot or blackcurrant jam. Cover with some of the Custard Cream, sandwich with remaining sponge. Cover sides and top with remaining custard cream and press meringue swirls to the sides and around the top edge.

CUSTARD CREAM

300ml (½ pint) milk
30ml (2 level tbsp) cornflour
225g (8oz) butter, softened
125g (4oz) caster sugar
2.5ml (½ tsp) vanilla flavouring

Blend some of the milk with the cornflour in a bowl. Boil the remaining milk, stir into the blended mixture. Return to the pan and stir over the heat until boiled and thickened. Place cling film on the custard and leave until cold. Beat together the butter, sugar and vanilla until soft and fluffy. Gradually beat in the cold custard. Chill slightly before spreading.

CHOCOLATE CAKES, CHERRY ALMOND CAKES, JAM OR CREAM FANCIES

4th Shelf

Paper Cases: Divide the remaining sponge mixture into three portions. To one portion, add 50g (2oz) chocolate dots. To one portion, add 40g (1½oz) chopped glacé cherries and a few drops of almond flavouring. Use the remaining portion plain. Fill the paper cases. Bake in the oven on the 4th shelf for about 15 minutes, until just firm to the touch. Cool on a wire rack. To finish the plain cakes, with a pointed small knife, cut out a shallow round from cake centre. Fill the hollows with jam or whipped fresh cream. Replace the cut out round and dredge with sifted icing sugar. Serve the chocolate and cherry cakes plain.

HOT SANDWICH PARTY

TUNA ROLLS
Tray 1. Serves 8

8 crisp bread rolls, white or wholemeal
297g (10½oz) canned tuna, drained
60ml (4 tbsp) chopped pickled gherkins
2 eggs, hard-boiled and chopped
75ml (5 level tbsp) mayonnaise
15ml (1 tbsp) lemon juice
15ml (1 tbsp) chopped fresh parsley
12 spring onions, trimmed
salt and pepper · 25g (1oz) butter, melted

Cut a slice from the top of each roll to make a lid. Scoop the crumbs from inside the rolls, leaving them hollow. Mix together the tuna, gherkins, eggs, mayonnaise, lemon juice and parsley. Reserve four spring onions for garnish. Chop the remainder and add to the tuna mixture with seasoning to taste. Fill the rolls with the mixture, put the lids on top and brush all over with the melted butter. Arrange the rolls on half of the oven tray. Bake in the oven on the 1st shelf for 10-15 minutes until the filling is hot. Slit the length of the green part of each spring onion and tuck under the lid as a garnish. Serve hot.

HAM AND CHEESE CROISSANTS
Tray 1

6 croissants
6 slices of ham · 7 slices of cheese
30ml (2 level tbsp) sweet pickle

Split the croissants, fill each with ham,* cheese and pickle. Top with remaining cheese slice cut in triangles. Bake with Tuna Rolls for 10-15 minutes until hot.

*Rolled to fit if necessary

FRENCH BREAD PIZZAS
Tray 2

50g (2oz) butter, softened
2.5ml (½ level tsp) dried oregano and basil mixed
1 or 2 garlic cloves, skinned and crushed
salt and pepper
one long French stick, split and cut into 6 pieces
2-3 large tomatoes, sliced
225g (8oz) Mozarella cheese, sliced
one 50g (2oz) can anchovy fillets, drained
6 black olives, halved and stoned

Mix together the butter, herbs, garlic and seasoning, and spread over each bread piece. Arrange the tomato then cheese slices on the bread. Split the anchovies lengthways, place on top of the cheese with the olives.

Arrange on one oven baking tray. Bake in the oven on the 3rd shelf for 10-15 minutes, until the cheese melts and bread is heated.

LIVER SAUSAGE SANDWICHES
Tray 3

225g (8oz) liver sausage, mashed
50g (2oz) butter, softened
30ml (2 level tbsp) corn or cucumber relish
5ml (1 tsp) Worcestershire sauce
10ml (2 level tsp) tomato ketchup
12 medium thin slices of wholewheat bread, crusts removed (optional)
stuffed olives, to garnish · salt & pepper

Mix together the liver sausage, 25g (1oz) of the butter, the corn or cucumber relish, Worcestershire sauce, ketchup and seasoning to taste. Spread the mixture over six slices of bread, sandwich together with the remaining slices. Spread the remaining butter on the outside of the sandwiches and arrange on half a baking tray with the Sausage Triangles. Bake in the oven on the 4th shelf for 10-15 minutes, turning once during baking until crisp and browned. Cut each sandwich in half, serve hot speared with stuffed olives on cocktail sticks.

SAUSAGE TRIANGLES
Tray 3

8 thin slices from large sandwich loaf, crusts removed
50g (2oz) butter, softened · salt and pepper
5ml (1 level tsp) wholegrain mustard
450g (1lb) pork sausages, cooked
8 pineapple cubes, drained and thinly sliced

Roll out the bread slices to flatten them. Mix together the butter, mustard and seasoning and spread on both sides of each bread slice. Place the sausages diagonally on the bread, add pineapple slices and roll the bread around the sausage, secure each with a cocktail stick. Arrange the triangles on half a tray with the Liver Sausage Sandwiches. Bake in the oven on the 4th shelf for 10-15 minutes, until the bread is crisp and browned. Serve hot speared with cocktail onions on sticks.

Fan oven only	
Temperature	180°C
Preheating	Not necessary
Shelf position	1st, 2nd, 4th
Time	10-15 minutes

THE MIELE COOK BOOK

INDEX

INDEX

Miele

AUSTRALIA
Miele Australia Pty Limited,
1 Gilbert Park Drive, Scoresby 3179.
PO Box 291, Ferntree Gully 3156 (Vic).
Tel: (03) 763 0066. Telex: 37747.

REPUBLIC OF IRELAND
Miele Ireland Limited, Sandyford Industrial Estate,
Foxrock, Dublin 18. Tel: 01-953109. Telex: 90099.

REPUBLIC OF SOUTH AFRICA
Miele (Pty) Limited, PO Box 1654, Randburg 2125,
304 Tungsten Road, Strydom Park, Ext 2, Randburg 2194.
Tel: (011) 793 7452. Telex: 4-27239.

UNITED KINGDOM
Miele Company Limited,
Fairacres, Marcham Road, Abingdon, Oxon. OX14 1TW
Tel: Abingdon (0235) 554455. Telex: 837121.

USA
Miele Appliances Inc,
22D Worlds Fair Drive, Somerset, New Jersey 08873.
Tel: (201) 560 0899.

Other Sales Companies

(A) Miele Ges.mbH, Wals/Salzburg,
Tel: (0662) 85 07 70 0.

(B) Miele NV, Asse/Mollem. Tel: (02) 452 87 00.

(CH) Miele AG, Spreitenbach/Zürich. Tel: 056 702 111.

(D) Miele & Cie – 4830 Gütersloh, West Germany.
Tel: (05241) 89 0.

(DK) Miele A/S, Glostrup/Copenhagen.
Tel: (02) 456611.

(E) Miele SA, Alcobendas/Madrid. Tel: (91) 652 86 00.

(F) Miele SA, Le Blanc-Mesnil/Paris Tel: (1) 4865 42 00.

(GR) Miele-Hellas GmbH, Athens. Tel: (01) 671 28 98.

(I) Miele GmbH, Eppan-St. Michael. Tel: (0471) 660066.

(L) Miele S.a.r.l. Luxembourg-Gasperich. Tel: 49 31 31.

(N) Miele A/S, Oslo. Tel: (02) 50 24 10.

(NL) Miele Nederland B.V. Vianen. Tel: (03473) 78 911.

(P) Miele Portuguesa Lda, Linda-A-Velha. Tel: (1) 21 88 544.

(S) Miele AB, Solna. Tel: (08) 7344900.

(SF) Miele OY, Helsinki. Tel: (90) 701 3001.